Edward Bond

# THE FOOL
## and
# WE COME TO THE RIVER

**EYRE METHUEN**

LONDON

# Contents

*First published 1976 by Eyre Methuen Ltd*
*11 New Fetter Lane London EC4P 4EE*
*© 1976 by Edward Bond*
*Printed in Great Britain by*
*Cox & Wyman Ltd, Fakenham, Norfolk*

ISBN 0413 34760 5 (Hardback)
ISBN 0413 34770 2 (Paperback)

# THE FOOL

*Scenes of Bread and Love*

# INTRODUCTION

## CAPITALISM

Not all communities have a culture. Some have only an organization. The members of an organization are often only monkey-people, who can organize and run advanced technologies and elaborate institutions and governments – but these things don't make a culture. An organization is concerned only with efficiency (though it is finally inefficient). Its technology tries to tell men how they can live. A culture does this too, but it also tells them how they ought to live and ensures that whatever is possible is done to make that ought practical; and the grounds for my optimism are that finally that is the only way men are content to live. Obviously we don't live in a culture. There is a discrepancy between what we have to do to keep our society running and what we're told we ought to do to be human. Our economy depends on exploitation and aggression. We expect business to be *ruthlessly* aggressive. At the same time we expect people to be generous and socially considerate. And we expect trade unionists to be dutiful workers and moderate in their demands – when they're at work. When they're consumers we expect them to be aggressive, to be competitive, greedy egotists – our way of life demands it. Advertising goads workers into needing more – *needing*, because its images are attached to human dignity, and so we need after-shave lotion for the reasons that we once needed salvation. Advertising tells the worker as consumer to be a master without responsibility to anyone but himself, a placid worker but a rampaging, selfish consumer demanding all the latest adult-toys and life-styles – which are his only rewards for reducing himself to a tool for two-thirds of his awake life. We're confronted with deep and destructive ironies: advertising is an incitement to strike and so capitalism destroys its organizational basis. We need anti-social behaviour to keep society running but this behaviour destroys society. The worker must 'know his place' in the factory but be an insatiable egotist outside it. The good citizen must be schizophrenic. And capitalism is incompatible with law and order. Ideally, capitalism would like to take a commodity out of one can – a tin – and put it into another can – a person. And although capitalism feeds on technocracy it is itself devoured by it, because technocracy destroys the acquiescing basis of society throughout the entire world – and while it grows rich on the poor it teaches them that the customer is always right.

Capitalism is competitive and its members use whatever power is at hand to extend and protect it. It's liberal, so far as it needs to protect itself from revolt, and when possible it substitutes affluence and moral and psychological pressure for force, because these are more easily justified and apparently (but only apparently) provoke less opposition. If it could supply enough goods, would it create complete satisfaction? No, it depends on dissatisfaction and by its nature it imposes the only means of meeting this dissatisfaction: consumer goods. Capitalism cannot satisfy the acquisitiveness it creates to maintain itself.

It tries to solve its dilemmas in many ways. Fascism is one way. It is the rational form of capitalism and tries to save it by consistency. This would work *if* we were prepared and able to behave permanently worse than animals. I say worse because animals are constrained by instincts and rigid physical limitations and men are not. But fascism can't have a culture because it's forced to equate that with driving people back to what it mistakenly regards as their instinctive nature.

Affluence is another attempt at salvaging capitalism. But this really only accelerates its decay. Affluence isn't well-being but a form of aggression. It makes consumption a form of competition. It makes the greedy hungry and the warm cold. Nothing is valued for itself but only for its consumption or possession. This is perpetually dissatisfying and the greater the dissatisfaction, the greater the business of stuffing things in the 'maw'. This can't create a culture because, firstly, it destroys its physical basis by squandering natural resources and in this way creates an ecological crisis in which we waste these resources to increase our dissatisfactions. And, secondly, because the more wealth that's put into the business of feverishly creating and stoking-up private dissatisfactions, the less there is to spend on the public fundamentals of culture or of any human society. The richer our organization becomes, the more impoverished are our schools, hospitals and welfare and social services. We abandon the old, we can't afford to socialize our children, our cities decay and our streets become the playground of violence, because we have neglected the necessities and decencies of life for the trivializing and ultimately despairing consumption of ersatz satisfactions. That is another irony: affluence impoverishes and produces the social conditions of scarcity.

## TECHNOLOGY

We fail to solve our problems because we're dazzled by our technology and think there's a scientific solution to everything. Neither technology nor science can by themselves or together create a culture. They can both be misused. Auschwitz and a hospital are both scientific-technological institutions. Our technology doesn't make us highly civilized. We live in a scientific barbarism, the most irrational society that's ever existed. A society's rationality isn't measured by what it knows or has, but by the use it makes of these things. Knowledge, technical skills – the more of these there are, the more crucial the question of use becomes. It's quite possible that in a rapidly developing technocracy the gap between society and reason may widen. How rational a community is it in which technology can imitate the Black Death and there are no reliable political or social safeguards to stop it? Or in which an audience can sit in a theatre while a few miles along the road men are sitting before the gadgets that fire nuclear weapons? Collectively we have never been so insecure. This doesn't mean that we can do without science – even to try would be barbarous. Science and technology are essential to our future. But left to the wrong people they can become a source of social irrationality. We need a culture that can use them wisely.

It's said that technocracy will usher in the age of freedom and real community because it will create such abundance that people won't need to compete and so their destructive human-animal nature will remain dormant. But technology by itself won't give us security through abundance. Apart from anything else society changes more slowly than technology, and so the gap between the initial successes of technology and its utopian apotheosis may be so great that it allows the irrationality of society to get out of hand and become so powerful that our species is destroyed. Technology can't produce utopia out of a hat. Culture must be fought for on its own ground as well. And cultural struggle, although of course it doesn't exist in a vacuum, can't be reduced to anything else. Without technology and science there could be no abundance, no welfare, no hope, no destruction of false myths. But without cultural struggle technocracy will be irrational and destructive. Morality can exist only in a culture or be forged in the quest for one. Outside that there are only superstitions, as in primitive societies, and hypocrisy, as in Western democracies.

Left to itself technology develops in relation to its own needs. 'Let's do X because it's possible to do it'. Of course X will be related to human needs, otherwise technology would exist in a vacuum, but human needs may increasingly be determined according to technological convenience. 'If there's a problem let's solve it in the way technology already knows. If there are many problems let's give them priorities based on present technological possibilities'. In this way technology may be progressing when human beings are only being processed. This has of course often happened in the past. But it becomes dangerous in an advanced technocracy. People must always be fitted into technological structures – rickets and other slum diseases have been among the negative signs of this – but now technology could go further, the tool could modify the user not in a real historical development but simply in an inhibition. The fantasy behind this is of Robots taking over. But you don't need Robots, you need only give the wrong priority to technology in general. We have to make choices about technology. These can only be properly made when they're guided by culture.

Human beings live by biological systems, most of which were developed and tested in lower animals. Evolution has been a self-disciplining system for millions of years. This has produced species that function well and relate well to their environment. We're living through fast technological and political changes and these must be constantly tested. Again, this can only be done properly in a culture.

## HUMAN NATURE

We don't have a fixed nature in the way other animals do. We have a 'gap' left by our freedom from the captive nature of other animals, from the tight control of instincts. The gap is filled by culture. Human nature is in fact human culture. The degree of culture is measured by its rationality. Rationality is the basis for discriminating between good and bad cultures. As human nature is human culture, human nature is social.

Men who live in an irrational society are driven to a kind of madness because such a society isn't in a static state, it deteriorates and ends by actively cultivating ignorance and combating knowledge. It can't be stabilized by its technology, however brilliant. On the contrary, its technology can be a danger. The neglect of social institutions, which I've already mentioned, affects us in many ways. It doesn't just divide individual against individual, it divides the individual against himself and tears him apart inwardly. An irrational man is frightened of himself as well as others. Irrationality is a state of *possession*. An animal doesn't know it's an animal but when men are irrational they know or sense that they are worse, more lost, than animals. They are not frightened of the strength and extent of their instincts – as it's often said – but of their weakness and limitation. A human being needs a culture to attach himself to real things in the outside world. When this doesn't happen, his unattached passions and emotions become self-parasitical. He either simply goes mad – and enters a state of false inventiveness which is unable to imagine the real (I shall try to explain this) because it finds it meaningless or unbearable – or he attaches his passions and emotions to substitute objects. He heaps possessions round him. He marks things as his possessions, his money, his property. Then the fulfilments of his passions are like crimes at the ends of cul de sacs. He is like a miser, he can never be rich, or like a glutton, he can never be fed, and he is cut off from creativity, which is the discovery of other people.

We need rationality not only to cope with our heightened self-consciousness, but also to answer questions about our existence. Everyone must answer some of these questions. Irrationality is never a harmless eccentricity. It is destructive. We don't have an animal nature which is violent, aggressive, egocentric, and which we must constantly fight in order to maintain a veneer of civilization. These destructive things are only *capacities*. We're born with many capacities and potentialities and these can be developed rationally so that we become socialized members of a culture. Disaster only occurs when we neglect to do this. Imagine a stack of bricks, floorboards, doors, tins of paint and bags of cement on a building site. They could be assembled into a strong, sound house. Instead they're left to rot and crumble. The glass is broken, the bags of cement ripped, it rains, weeds grow over the heap and then the rats move in. We didn't build Auschwitz because our animal natures made us do it, but because we neglected to create our nature.

Capitalism uses force and morality to try to restrain change, but it can't. Not only does it destroy its social basis and the characters of its members, it is itself destroyed by its own myths. An irrational organization needs myths to maintain itself. In this it's unlike culture, which seeks truth. Obvious myths are, from the past, the dogma of original sin, and in our day the dogma of original violence – the idea that violence is a necessity of human nature in the way eating and sleeping are, and not just a capacity such as fear or pain. Both these myths have been used to justify force to preserve social relationships. As the toys of affluence become brighter and faster and noisier, so it becomes necessary for capitalism to take an increasingly pessimistic view of human nature. Original violence is, of course, a far more pessimistic doctrine than original sin because there is no redemption in earth *or* heaven. This increasing pessimism isn't accidental. Capitalism creates a schizophrenic society of tension and aggression, and because 'consumerism' can't calm or restrain this (on the contrary), so more force and control and scrutiny are necessary. Authoritarianism and myth will penetrate deeper into human and social relations, not because capitalism can't imagine other methods and dream of different horizons, but because it's unable to achieve them. When conservatives ask for more privacy they only want it, like the burglar, for business hours.

If human nature is a vacuum waiting to be filled by culture, not a tabula rasa but a set of biological expectations, and if these expectations aren't met, then not only do people become haunted by disembodied passions in the way I've described, but whole societies are condemned to live out the myths they create to maintain their injustice. Our myth is that we are essentially violent but that there are scientific and technological means of controlling our violence – and we live out our myth by creating the weapons of death. In this way the first world war can be seen as the myth of the nineteenth century. The dreams of the old enlightenment have been lost and we see our society becoming more violent, despairing and uncultured. Science in the service of profiteering won't create a new enlightenment. We won't achieve that till we change our political and social basis. And in passing I would add that the idea of a society of hedonists stimulated (or is it pacified?) by a technology of lights, smells, sounds and feels – that is pure science fiction, based on the illusion that to be happy we have only to satisfy our instincts. The bright people would murder one another on the streets, and they wouldn't wait for the cover of darkness.

Animal instincts are concerned with survival, and as men aren't guided through life by instincts, they have no alternative, if they're going to survive, but to understand their lives. If they refrain or are prevented from doing this, then their condition is as absurd as a dog's would be if it could ignore its instincts. Such a man would be very like a dog chained up and starved. The dog dies because its need for food has a direct relation to an appropriate activity, eating, and if this doesn't occur the need is removed: the dog dies. But if a man's need for a rational understanding isn't met, the end is postponed, because the man must invent something to meet the need. The object of any biological structure is to orientate itself and perpetuate its kind. For man this means the need to relate himself to society, his individuality to the community, and to observe the relationship. When a man can't do this, his passions and emotions turn inward, in the way I've described, and relate only to himself. He invents a fantasy reality. He's like a chained dog who takes to devouring himself. Such a man soon pulls reality down on his head, and whole classes do the same.

## CULTURE

Culture is the rational creation of human nature, the implementation of rationality in all human activity, economic, political, social, public and private. A culture must unite technology, science, and political and economic organization, and relate them to our environment in such a way that we can continue our lives and broaden them socially and humanely. It must show us how we can live and how we ought to live so that there is a future for us. When it uses myth it does so not for Plato's reasons, but as working hypotheses in matters not yet fully understood. Our species must order its nature rationally because irrationality is a state of accelerating decay leading to destruction. Even if this were not so, a man left to his instincts could still only use a small number of his potential abilities. He might grub for roots for a while but he could never build a farm. Instincts can't produce culture. Culture is built into the gap in human nature – the open brain, the awareness that develops itself exponentially, the capacity for thought that needs to learn in both a disciplined and a playful way.

How does the artist help to create culture? Technology says what's workable, and politics what's possible, at a particular time. And as most scientists aren't mad, and most politicians aren't power maniacs, the artist can understand political necessity and sympathize with political compromise, just as much as he enjoys the benefits of technology. But culture isn't made from these things alone. Everyone has a creative imagination, the faculty that's used, among other things, to create and understand art. I think that creative imagination is related to rationality and through this to human values. I don't know of any fascist 'art' – book, film, picture or anything else – that isn't tawdry and ludicrous. I shall say more about art later. Here I want to stress that it can only be rational and have a social meaning and purpose.

Just as culture is the way a society meets its fundamental needs, and not something it adds later, so it isn't a veneer a well-fed, secure person adds to his life as a luxury. Culture is what he is and what will become of him. It is the cause and consequence of his daily life. Art helps to monitor the creation of culture and reflects the past and future in the present. Without some form of creative imagination we probably can't be human beings at all, not because we wouldn't be nice and civilized but because we couldn't function biologically in such a way as to remain sane and create a future for our species. Creative imagination is a necessary element in culture, and without it we are denatured animals without even the security of belonging to nature: not a species being shaped by natural selection, but the victims of a vicious chaos *we* have created.

Art is usually taken to be a very private experience. This goes back to the nineteenth century, the first age that tried to take art away from the masses of people. The nineteenth century pursued a lop-sided development, not the mutual cooperation of technology, politics and art, which is essential to culture. Of course most art falls short of its aim. But the honesty of its aim can be recognized in its intellectual rigour, and because nothing false is added to heighten or sensationalize it. There is a specialism in art just as there is in technology and politics. It only becomes embarrassing when the artist suggests he's a specialist in another, finer world. He's a specialist in describing this world, and all art is realism. We're the product of material circumstances and there's no place in art for mysticism or obscurantism. Art is the illustration, illumination, expression of rationality – not something primitive, dark, the primal urge or anything like that. Science can work irrationally but art never can, because it must always show what it is doing. Its truth is written on its face. That *is* art. But we must learn how to look, and teaching about art is as important as creating it. The S S Commandant didn't read Goethe, he admired himself reading Goethe.

Art can't be judged by the literal images it creates – that's the danger of propaganda whether of the Royal Academy or the Left. Surely most artists know of circumstances in which they'd want to produce propaganda of the directest, simplest sort? Propaganda can be good art. Looked at properly a Rembrandt portrait is a propaganda poster. But propaganda ceases to be art when it becomes the mechanical duplication of images. Then it trivializes the information it conveys and can produce bewilderment.

Sincerity is a necessary element in art, and the contemporary religious artist in a revolutionary state may be sincere. But kitsch is also sincere. Art is finally judged not on its sincerity but on its rationality. Well, if art is rational, it clearly can't be judged solely by what it criticizes. It must show the standards by which it criticizes, and these must be illustrated in the work of art. To say 'X is wrong', in the perpetual crisis of political necessity, isn't enough. The right course or emphasis must be illustrated. Art is responsible for the relation between the present and its vision, and this has to be shown in the work of art or its utopia becomes kitsch. We must be able to recognize ourselves somewhere in the people in the artist's utopia, and to relate its freedom to our necessity. Politics can be escapist, technology can, but art never can. The artist can't create a utopia and oppose that abstractly to the present. He must explain on the surface of his art the relationship between his utopia and the present. If he is a religious artist he must explain what god is up to now – and this means that in our age religious art is in fact anti-religious or kitsch.

Art isn't just the articulation of utopia, or even a foretaste of it. It also helps to monitor the consequence of change. Outside utopia art can be critical. The aim of this criticism is to ensure that the necessities of the present don't reproduce the future in their own image. To put it in contemporary jargon, part of culture is feedback. A society that excluded the critical part of creative imagination would *pharaohize* itself. I'm not asking for the voice of the individual against the collective, but in what way can each individual learn how to speak for the collective? We can't function efficiently as ant-like units in an organization, because each of us carries the whole community in himself. We must represent it, not just belong to it. Human nature is culture, and culture is social because it develops through social experience and practice. So human nature is social nature or (as I've said) worse than animal. Our species has a future only as a self-conscious collective, and this will extend the individual self-consciousness which has developed in the past. Culture will be each individual's understanding of his community and his commitment to it.

## WHAT IS ART?

I've given some indication of what I think the artist's role should be, and of what society should ask from him. I would like to be able to answer the old question 'What is art?' more fully, but I can only offer the inadequate suggestions that occurred to me when I wrote *The Fool* – and even these are really questions rather than answers. Nowadays art is often dismissed as irrelevant to the solution of social problems. It will be clear that I don't believe this. If creative imagination exists in all people, it must have a use. It's too potent, and in the past has been too effective, to be an accident of nature.

Our whole biological being is a means of orientating and perpetuating ourselves. So our passions and emotions are part of the means of doing this, and of obtaining knowledge of the world (especially in the sense of 'canny' knowledge or insight), just as much as our five senses are. And the same is true of our creative imaginations. (Whether creative imagination is a separate faculty, or the effect of the working of other faculties, doesn't matter.)

The 'gap' in our natures is filled by our understanding and experience of the world. This understanding and experience make us what we are, and what we are can be either chaotic or rationally ordered. If it's rationally ordered, it is a culture (or is involved in creating a culture). A culture isn't just an assemblage of knowledge, because in the context of culture what we know becomes the ground for action. It's a way of recognizing the world which involves both our emotions and our rational minds. A simple metaphor (not in anyway literal) is that of the 'gap' as a stomach, the stomach walls as emotions and reason as the digestive juice. This metaphorical stomach works on what is put into it and creates a sane culture – an emotionally evaluated, rational understanding of the world. It is the individual's summing up or balancing of himself as a relationship between the world, his society, and his instinctive capacities. It is a human being's intellectual and canny knowledge of reality – but he has built reality through his creative imagination, not merely observed it or borne its brunt. It is a process of self-creation. The result can be intellectual or simple, but not stupid. Art is the images, sounds, dynamics of this rational process of creation – and that's why I say that art is the imagination of the real and not the invention of fantasy. If, on the other hand, the process is passive, because the individual is paralysed by neglect, fear, or anything else, then a culture is not created.

Creative imagination need not always be expressed in art – there are other expressions of it – but it must be expressed in art sometimes. The artist's job is to make the process public, to create public images, literal or figurative, in sight, sound and movement, of the human condition – public images in which our species recognizes itself and confirms its identity. There are obvious parallels with species-identification in other animals, but art, by being associated with rationality and value, goes further than these.

Art is a direct record of the creation of human nature. It places the individual in the world, and interprets the world in accordance with possibilities and human needs. It expresses the real within the limits of knowledge at a particular time and in this way it has always been rational, even when this meant dancing for the rain.

The artist should look as closely and comprehensively as he can at the developing creation of human nature, and do this without excuse or fear and without being gratuitously shocking. The complexity is usually in the skill, the vision should be simple; it gets some of its strength from the absence of illusion. Art helps to create meaning and purpose in what is in many ways an apparently irrational world. In a culture, or the struggle for a culture, a cry, a tear, a death become rational. Art is beautiful only in the broadest sense because it can include death and ugliness. But it can never commit itself to despair or the irrational. Art is the human being claiming a rational relationship with the world, perhaps even especially when what it portrays might have otherwise seemed absurd or tragic. No one can look questioningly at a work of art and not be made freer, even when faced with promethean necessity and when making those judgments that turn into calculations.

The last scene of *The Fool* is set in an asylum. In this scene I've tried to show that rational processes were still being worked out even in the apparently insane world of nineteenth-century Europe. The English slums of that time were like slow-motion concentration camps – death takes longer in slums than in concentration camps. Art has always looked at the atrocities of the age in which it was created. What Adorno and Auden said about poetry and Auschwitz misses the point. They would have hit it only if Auschwitz had been the summing up of history – and of course it wasn't.

*for Irene*

*The Fool* was first performed at the Royal Court Theatre on 18 November 1975 with the following cast:

JOHN CLARE Tom Courtenay
MILES David Troughton
DARKIE Nigel Terry
LAWRENCE Mick Ford
PATTY Bridget Turner
MARY Caroline Hutchison
LORD MILTON Nicholas Selby
THE PARSON John Normington
LORD MILTON'S GUESTS
   Peter Myers
   John Boswall
   Malcolm Ingram
   Robert Lloyd
   Shiela Kelley
   Avril Marsh
WADLOW, LORD MILTON'S
   GAMEKEEPER Roger Hume
HILARY, THE ASSISTANT KEEPER
   David Ellison
BOB Roderick Smith
PETER Malcolm Ingram
BETTY Shiela Kelley
HAMO Brian Hall
GENTLEMEN Peter Myers,
   Robert Lloyd, John Boswall

HICKS, A WARDER Tony Rohr
GOVERNOR Peter Myers
PORTER Ken Gajadhar
JACKSON Brian Hall
PORTER'S BACKERS
   Malcolm Ingram, Mick Ford
JACKSON'S BACKERS
   David Troughton
   Roger Hume
REFEREE David Ellison
A BOY Roderick Smith
MRS EMMERSON Isabel Dean
CHARLES LAMB Robert Lloyd
MARY LAMB Gillian Martell
ADMIRAL LORD RADSTOCK
   Bill Fraser
DR SKRIMSHIRE John Boswall
TOMMY Tony Rohr
MICHAEL Roger Hume
ARNY Brian Hall
NAPOLEON John Normington
A MAN IN A STRAITJACKET
   Mick Ford
AN ATTENDANT David Troughton

Directed by Peter Gill
Designed by William Dudley

*One:* The porch of Lord Milton's house; *Two:* A wood near Helpstone; *Three:* A lane at Littleport; *Four:* A cell at Ely; *Five:* Hyde Park; *Six:* Clare's garden; *Seven:* Open ground; *Eight:* A drawing room
*There is an interval after Scene Four*
*Note:* In Scene Five the fight is played simultaneously with the rest of the action. The placing of the rounds is the one used at the first production. In the same production the mummers' parts in Scene One were played in this way:

Enterer-in — MILES
St George — LAWRENCE
Bullslasher — DARKIE
Doctor — CLARE

# SCENE ONE

*Porch of* LORD MILTON's *house. Winter. Evening.*

*A bench.*

CLARE, DARKIE, LAWRENCE *and* MILES *come on. They are dressed as mummers. They carry lanterns.* PATTY *follows them.*

CLARE. We'll start then.

    CLARE *knocks on the door.*

MILES. Hear anythin', boy?

CLARE. Howd your row so's I can listen. (*Knocks.*) Summat's comin'.

> *The door opens.* MARY *stands in the doorway. She is dressed as kitchen staff.*

MARY. On't hev t'knock our door down old chap. (*Laughs.*) You do look a spectacle.

> MARY *goes back into the house. She shuts the door.*

DARKIE. Shut door smart so's you on't git a proper see in.

PATTY. On't start.

MILES. Who told you t'come gall?

PATTY. Told meself.

LAWRENCE. Thass lads only t'night.

MILES. Know what she's after.

PATTY. T'on't you.

DARKIE. None on us ought-a come.

MILES. Lordship allus give us silver.

DARKIE (*knocking*). Waitin' all night.

PATTY (*sudden warning*). On't shout down the keyhole boy!

> MARY *opens the door.*

MARY. Told you not t'knock. Housekeeper'll send you packin' lads.

DARKIE. Howd your row woman.

MILES. Thass Christmass. On't hev no rows.

    MARY *laughs at their costumes. She goes back into the house. She shuts the door behind her.*

LAWRENCE (*looking through the keyhole*). Drat great roomy old place. (*Sudden warning.*) Hey up!

    *The* MUMMERS *line up.*

PATTY. Goo hot when he look at me.

    *The* MEN *laugh nervously. The door opens.* LORD MILTON, PARSON *and a few* LADIES *and* GENTLEMEN *come on to the porch.* LORD MILTON *is a giant. The* MUMMERS *raise their lanterns and bow.*

MUMMERS (*chorus*). Please you t'want the mummers this season a good will my lord.

MILTON. Welcome at Christmas tide good friends.

    MILTON, *his family and guests hiss, boo, laugh and whistle in response to the mumming. They hold glasses and empty them, but they are not refilled.*

## The Play

ENTERER IN.
    We hope your favour we shall win
    For acting time is come and we appear
    Let merriment begin
    This joyful time a year
    We are not of the ragged sort
    But some of the royal trim,
    An if you on't heed what *I* say
    Let Saint George enter in.
        *Enter* SAINT GEORGE.

ST GEORGE.
    I am Saint George the parfick knight
    An this is my golden sword.
    I met the dragon in terrible fight

An killed him as you've heard.
England's Champion am I
An anyman here I do defy.

*Enter* COLONEL BULLSLASHER.

BULLSLASHER.
I am Colonel Bullslasher
Otherwise known as Boney.
This is my crusher an basher an hasher
I'll kill Saint George an take his money.

*They roar and fight.* SAINT GEORGE *is wounded.*

MILTON. Carrie stand out of the wind.

*A* GENTLEMAN *puts a shawl round a lady's shoulders.*

ST GEORGE.
O pardon Saint George the parfick knight
For he is wounded sore.
BULLSLASHER.
I will not pardon you Saint George
I'll kill you ten times more.

COLONEL BULLSLASHER *kills* SAINT GEORGE.

ENTERER IN.
Alas Saint George you hev died this day.
By Colonel Bullslasher slain.
In the cold earth you will lay.
Your friends are left in ruin.

*Enter the* DOCTOR.

DOCTOR. I am the Doctor.
ENTERER IN. Doctor can you cure this man?
DOCTOR. Ten pound if he's rich, twenty pound if he's poor.
ENTERER IN. He's very poor.
DOCTOR.
I've a bottle of pills from my auntie in Spain.
They are good for the wind an' better for rain.

I cured a squire who neighed like a horse.
Now he bray like a donkey an he's very much worse.
The queen had a fit so I gave her a pill.
She never felt better an' she's constantly ill.
Saint George here is my magical potion-lotion-notion
    commotion. Take ten drops on a fork an' stir it with a knife.
Then see what my brew
Can doo for you.

*The* DOCTOR *pours a bottle down* ST GEORGE'S *throat.* ST
GEORGE *stands.*

ST GEORGE.
Hello good people, now give three cheer!
The like was never seen –
When I died I had my seven wits
An now I hev seventeen.

*Song and dance:*

*Hal-an-tow.*

Where are the Spaniards
That made so great a boast-o?
For they shall eat the grey goose feather
An we shall eat the roast-o.
    Hal-an-tow jolly rumble-o
    For we were up as soon as any day-o
    An for to sing for summer come
    The summer an the may-o
    For summer will a-come-o
    The winter will a-goo-o.

As for Saint George-o
Saint George he was a knight-o
Of all the knights in christendom
St George he has the right-o
In every land-o
The land where'er we go
    Hal-an-tow etc.

God bless Aunt Mary Moses

With all her power and might-o
An send us peace in Merry England
Both by night an day-o
In every land-o
The land that e'er we go
    Hal-an-tow etc.

PATTY.   &#125;
MILES.   &#125;    Wren. Wren.

*Others, including the people on the porch, shout* 'The Wren'.
'Hunting the Wren'.

THE MUMMERS (*sing*).

### Hunting the Wren

We'll hunt the wren says Robin the bobbin,
We'll hunt the wren says Richie the robin,
We'll hunt the wren says Jack a the land,
We'll hunt the wren says everyone.
Where o where? says Robin the bobbin,
Etc.
In yonder green bush says Robin the bobbin,
Etc.
How git him down says Robin the bobbin,
Etc.
With sticks an' stones says Robin the bobbin.
Etc.
How'll we eat him? says Robin the bobbin,
Etc.
With knives an' forks says Robin the bobbin,
Etc.
Eyes to the blind says Robin the bobbin,
Legs to the lame says Richie the robin,
Scraps to the poor says Jack a the land,
Bones to the dogs says everyone.

The wren the wren is king a the birds,
Saint Stephen's Day he's caught in the furze,
Although he is little his family is great,
We pray yoo good people to give us a treat.

*The hat has been passed round. Applause.*

MILTON. A fine Saint George and a terrible Bullslasher.

GENTLEMAN. Try my gout on that doctor.

PARSON. In this year of our lord eighteen hundred and fifteen England is beset by troubles. The tyrant Bonaparte has been put down. But we are entering a new age. An iron age. New engines, new factories, cities, ways, laws. The old ways must go. The noble horse and the hand are slow. Our land must be better used. Forests cut down. Open spaces put to the plough. All of us must be patient and understanding. We must work for the common good. God bless you.

DARKIE. On't heard you give a sermon afore parson.

PARSON. Come to church and you would.

DARKIE. Too tired. Sit on me arse after work not me knees. I'd fall asleep an' they'd blame your sermon!

PARSON. Well it's Christmas so you're pleased to joke.

DARKIE. On't pleased at nothing. My Christmas's spuds an' greens.

*The* LADIES *go into the house.*

MILTON. The war made us all prosperous but prices have fallen with the peace. Wages must follow. Not because I say so. That is a law of economic science. Wages follow prices or civil institutions break down. Civilization costs money like everything else. Put too much in your own pockets and what's left to pay for our state institutions? Well, now you have something to think about. They'll give you hot pies and punch in the kitchen. Thank you for your play. Goodnight.

MILTON *and the* GENTLEMEN *go into the house.*

PARSON. You offended his lordship Turner.

MILES. On't mean no damage sir. Allus talk straight out. Worried for his old ma. She hev t'give up work on the land. Lad his age ought-a git married. But thass on'y takin a woman in t'beggary!

PARSON. I'm surprised at the turn this festivity's taken. Our rulers guide our affairs in such a way that each of us reaps the

best possible reward for his labours. Without their guidance –
though you might not understand it – there'd be chaos.

DARKIE. We're headed that way now.

PARSON. Turner, Christmas is the gift of god. A time as serene
as this night sky. Can nothing lighten your dark spirit?

LAWRENCE. Hard times all round.

PARSON. My prayers will be very long tonight. All of you have
friends Turner. We shall come through. Let that be the Lord's
will.

DARKIE. Six day a week I goo t'work in the dark an' come home
in the dark – for what? Ten shillin'. Even Judas got thirty – but
he come from a good family an' wouldn't work for less.

PARSON. Goodnight.

*The* PARSON *goes into the house.* MARY *shuts the door from the
inside.* DARKIE *sits on the bench.*

PATTY. Let's goo round the kitchen. Warm there.

DARKIE (*puts his head in his hands*). His drink'd choke me.

CLARE. Can't afford t'feel like that boy. Spite yourself. (*To*
MILES.) Goo an' fetch it. I'll kip an eye on him.

LAWRENCE *and* MILES *go out.* PATTY, CLARE *and* DARKIE
*are left.* CLARE *sits on the bench beside* DARKIE.

PATTY. Serve you right Darkie. My feet's froze. Upset everyone
else an' end up upset yourself! Well thass Christmas, I on't
goo on. Sit yourself up boy an' look on the bright side. No
crack heads yit.

DARKIE *doesn't move.*

CLARE. He all right?

PATTY. Pay no notice.

PATTY *sits between* CLARE *and* DARKIE. DARKIE *stays
completely motionless. He has his head in his hands.*

PATTY (*to* CLARE). Cold hands, boy! (*Laughs.*)

CLARE (*puts his arms round her*). You look all right – (*Puts his
hand in her dress.*)

PATTY. What yoo lost, boy?

CLARE (*feeling her breasts*). Togged up special t'set me on.

PATTY. On't need settin' on. Git that all the time when we're wed. On't hev t'kip grabbin' –

CLARE. On't mind grabbin'.

PATTY (*giggling as* CLARE *unbuttons her*). Darkie make your mate behave.

> DARKIE *remains motionless.*

CLARE (*nodding towards the house*). Hush.

PATTY. When we're wed –

CLARE. On't rush in t'weddin'. Hev t'afford a wife an' family fore I wed.

> DARKIE *doesn't move.* MILES *and* LAWRENCE *come back. They carry mugs, a jug and pies.*

MILES. Is his lordship hangin' out the winder? Darkie your mate hev his hand up your sister's dress.

LAWRENCE. Knew what she come after.

PATTY (*taking* CLARE'*s hands away and buttoning her clothes. Nods at* DARKIE). Sulks. Told him off. What they give us?

LAWRENCE. Hot punch.

PATTY. Drunk half hev you?

MILES (*pouring*). Left you a drop in the bottom.

> *They drink.*

All the best.

CLARE. Health and wealth.

PATTY. O – good drop a stuff.

DARKIE (*drinking*). Thanks all round to his lordship.

> *The door opens.* MARY *comes out.*

MARY. On't allowed make that row out here.

PATTY. On't heard no row gall.

MARY. That chair on't for sittin' on this time a night neither. We're lock up. You're supposed t'goo round the back.

DARKIE (*to* MARY). On't got no quarrel with you gall. (*Turns to the others.*) She's just an ijit.

MILES. Git off home, mates.

> MILES, LAWRENCE *and* DARKIE *go.* MARY *goes in and shuts the door.* PATTY *watches her.*

CLARE. Run them round the back. I'll howd on an' see you home.

> PATTY *takes mugs and jugs off.* CLARE *is alone. He stands and stares at the door. He puts his hand on his crutch. The door opens slightly.* MARY *comes out. She stays by the door.*

MARY. What you watchin'?

CLARE. Come over here.

MARY. On't try your tricks on me. Saw you with your gall.

CLARE. On't my gall.

MARY. On't look like it.

CLARE. She'll be back soon.

MARY. O ay.

CLARE (*still holding his crutch*). When they let you out?

MARY. All accordin'.

CLARE. Hev t'walk her home. Said I would. When'll I see you?

MARY. Depend.

CLARE. When?

MARY On't promise. (*Beckons with her head.*) Hall's dark though.

> CLARE *follows her into the house. She shuts the door behind them.* PATTY *comes on.*

PATTY. Look at the stars boy. All them. Bet people goo t'school ten year an' still can't count so far. (*Looks round.*) Boy? (*Pause.*) Drat!

> PATTY *hurries out after the others.*

## SCENE TWO

*Wood. Night.*

CLARE *alone. He sits. His lips move and his fingers tap a rhythm. He is saying something noiselessly to himself. He has a piece of paper in his hand but he doesn't read it. Suddenly he turns his head.*

PATTY *comes in.*

PATTY. I know what's gooin' on.

CLARE. Bats up there. Hundreds an' hundreds. Listen. Sky full.

PATTY. Creepin' round the wood at night. On't born yesterday.

PATTY *starts to cry. Slight pause.*

CLARE. There! – they've gone. Great hole gapin' right on top of us. You cry like a bat gall. Driv 'em off.

PATTY. Know sort a gall meet fellas out here. Cost more'n you've got. Gloves an' hankies. An' you on't git nothin' worth hevin'. My head screw on I'd let you git on with it. Learn you a lesson. (*Pause.*) Us'll git along all right. Make a good wife s'long's you behave.

CLARE. I know.

PATTY. On't want no one bar you. Never hev since I set eyes on you. On't ashamed a that, thass just a fact. Wish I had a kid. We'd hev t'git wed then.

CLARE. On't you goo on gall!

PATTY. On't force you. You on't keen, we'll let the matter drop.

CLARE. On't be daft gall.

PATTY. On't hev that flung in me face every time there's a row: you had your arm twist. Goo off with some gall if thass what you want. On'y on't live my end the village. On't want see the two of you every time I goo t'the winder.

CLARE. You doo goo on gall!

PATTY. Just sayin' so it's understood. (CLARE *kisses her.*) My ma think good on you John. Say you on't be no trouble outside the drink. Thass a question of can us afford it? Like a drop myself as you know. But I *on't* howd with wastin' flesh on drink when you on't afford t'eat. On't see the –

CLARE. On't *drink*. Likely I had you t'come home to I on't touch a drop gall.

PATTY. Now on't start putting that on me. I on't say give up. Man's a man. Thass a question a lettin' your glass empty afore your purse.

DARKIE *comes in,*

PATTY. Well I'll goo t'buggery. You allus follow us boy.

DARKIE. On't follow you. Come after John.

PATTY. How'd you know where we were?

DARKIE. Bin up his house.

CLARE. What's up boy?

DARKIE. I wondered hev you heard? They're cuttin' the forest down t'make fields.

CLARE. What boy?

DARKIE. Milton want the land for corn.

CLARE. Why's that?

DARKIE. Sell t'the old factory boys. They on't grow corn.

CLARE. But not *so* much!

DARKIE. Ay. More. They'll drain the common fen an' turn off the river.

CLARE. Thass a lot a old scare talk.

PATTY (*nervously*). Thass true boy. They saw chaps gooin' round the fields this mornin with chains an' writin' books. Thass how it all come out. Wrote the river down in the books.

DARKIE. An' the forest.

CLARE. *You* heard a this gall? (*She nods.*) How'd you git rid of a river – (*Laughs.*) turn the river off!

PATTY. Dam her up an' pump her out boy!

CLARE. Can't – thass our's much as his. An' the fens. An' the trees. What's it mean boy? We'll lose our fishin' – our wood – cows on the fen common. How'll we live? Not on the few bob they pay us for workin' their land. We need us own bit a land.

DARKIE. They take all the land they'll hev t'pay us proper wages.

CLARE. Like factory boys? They git proper wages?

DARKIE. Ah ... An' I said my piece too often. On't even offer me work.

PATTY. On't howd that agin you.

DARKIE. No?

PATTY. Talk's no harm. They – (*She stops.*) You bin up t'summat?

DARKIE. No.

PATTY. Fightin'!

DARKIE. Push. Thass all.

PATTY. Who? Who?

DARKIE. Milton's gaffer.

PATTY (*frightened*). O you bloody fool boy!

DARKIE. Ask him what his chaps were up to with chains an' books. Took howd a my coat. I say I on't your cattle boy! Push, thass all. Goo down so's he could say I hit him. On't stun a fly.

PATTY. Doo ma know? (DARKIE *shrugs*.) I'll soon tell her. Rowin', fightin' – thass all you know about Darkie. She'll hev summat t' say.

DARKIE. Say what her like.

CLARE. Give over rowin'.

DARKIE. Rowin'? Wait till you wed her – then you'll know what rowin' is! I'm sick a rowin'. Allus rowin'.

PATTY. Whose fault's that?

DARKIE. O Patty you know ma's like an adder gooin' for a stoat.

PATTY. On't ought a say that.

DARKIE. You know it's true. She hev her reasons. On't easy bringin' up hungry kids. That on't make her easier t'live with now we're growed up.

> The KEEPER *comes in. He wears a dark suit and cap. He carries a gaming gun.*

KEEPER. What you up to in this wood?

CLARE. Walkin'.

KEEPER. Trespassin'.

PATTY. On't come so soft boy. Allus use this wood.

DARKIE. Who're you?

KEEPER. Lord Milton's keeper.

CLARE. On't got no keeper s'far's I heard.

KEEPER. Hev ten now.

CLARE. This on't private land. If that was we still hev rights a way.

KEEPER. Move on, there's good lads. New here. On't want start trouble. An' you ought a be home makin' your old people easy miss. Know the sort a gall goo out with two lads this time a night.

DARKIE. Yoo jump out a cess pit! You're fit t'be Lord Milton's keeper.

KEEPER. What's your name lad?

PATTY (*to* DARKIE). No boy! You come home with me. 'Nough trouble for one day!

DARKIE (*to* KEEPER). You on't last long in this village boy!

KEEPER. On't in village. Live on estate.

PATTY (*to* DARKIE). You come home. (*To* CLARE.) An' you John. Straight home. I'll come round t'morra.

> DARKIE *and* PATTY *go out right.* CLARE *out left.*

KEEPER. Want keepers a people round here.

> *The* KEEPER *follows* DARKIE *and* PATTY *off. Almost immediately* MARY *comes on.*

DARKIE (*off*). On't walk back a me pointin' your gun boy. On't a criminal yet.

> CLARE *comes on. He stands some way away from her.*

MARY. Saw me in the trees on't you.

CLARE. Bin here night after night.

MARY. Housekeeper saw you playin' with yourself. Crep' up on the landin and watch. Jealous old bitch. Say I on't fit for servants' hall. Threw me out. After prayers next mornin'.

CLARE. Waited every night. All hours. For weeks.

MARY. On't hev no proper job now. Old cow warned all the big houses. Got in with some travellers.

CLARE. Gypsies?

MARY. T'on't your fault. On't last *there*. Done a violence with the silver cutlery fore long. Git a lot more laughs now. On'y I on't sure bout the winter yit. Saw your gall.

CLARE. Her brother took her home.

MARY. Thought he was her fella way he was gooin'. Keep an eye on you doo he?

CLARE. No life campin' in ditches.

MARY (*sits*). I live with one a the gypsy bosses. Keeper on his rounds.

CLARE. Soon tell him t'bugger off. (*Squats beside her but doesn't touch her.*) On't bin out my head. That night. Never forget you.

MARY. Hungry?
CLARE. Allus hungry.

> MARY *takes out bread and gives him some. They eat.*

MARY. Stole it.
CLARE (*touches her breast while he eats*). Well built gall. Never seen a gall like you. Like t'live in this forest. The two on us. Tread the reeds an' creep in.
MARY. Damp. Gypsies know better'n that.

> CLARE *pushes her onto the ground.*

All right.

> *Off,* KEEPER *whistles. One short blast.*

MARY. Shall us wait?
CLARE. Come on.

> *A young* ASSISTANT KEEPER *comes on left.*

KEEPER (*off*). Hilary?
ASSISTANT KEEPER. Hear that Mr Waddlow? (*Points.*) There.

> KEEPER *comes on right.*

KEEPER. Galls. On't git caught up Hilary. Hev you down here while their husbands robbin' the hatches.
MARY (*quietly to* CLARE). Goo on.
ASSISTANT KEEPER (*points*). There Mr Wadlow.
KEEPER. Let him draw her boy. Never drive that out the wood. Animal in rut. Under your feet, step over 'em, worms rolled up, birds gallivantin', fishes on top a each other. Gills goo as if they're drownin'.
ASSISTANT KEEPER (*hears something*). Again Mr Wadlow.
KEEPER. Sights I've seen. (*Laughs.*) Chop rabbits down while they do it in the graveyard. Seen two stoats at it in a broken gravestone.
CLARE (*quietly*). Bugger's mad.
ASSISTANT KEEPER (*points*). There.

> MARY *and* CLARE *groan.*

KEEPER (*calls*). On't waste a shell! (*To* ASSISTANT KEEPER.) Think a the cost. Hev a skin t'show each time you shoot. (*He reaches the* ASSISTANT KEEPER'*s side*.) Git the vermin gibbets up t'morra. Keep a good line a carcas hung up. Old crows, rats, owl. Boss creep round on the sly an' count the corpses. Check up you're keepin' busy. Show you how t'fix em so they on't drop off when they rot.

   *The* KEEPERS *go out.*

CLARE. Bugger's gone.

MARY (*quietly amused. Looks down at her crotch*). You made little drops on my hair. Silver in this moonlight.

CLARE. On't goo.

   MARY *stands. She and* CLARE *fasten their clothes.*

MARY. My boss is waitin'.

CLARE. Don't.

MARY. Come back your place then?

CLARE. Well. (MARY *laughs*). Yes. Us'll manage. There's on'y my old people.

MARY. Rather be stoned out the village than look down on respectable. Your gall on't put out the flags neither. 'Night boy.

CLARE. Us'll work out summat.

MARY. What?

CLARE. Marry me.

MARY. On't talk so far back.

CLARE. What you called gall?

MARY. Mary if you must know.

CLARE. Where's your camp?

MARY. On't hev you there.

CLARE. You be here t'morra night or I'll come round.

MARY. Git a crack head.

CLARE. I'll walk you back.

MARY. Bugger off if you want t'see me t'morra.

CLARE. They move camp where'll you goo?

MARY. On't tell me. Move sharp sometime. Folk come out an' stone us off.

CLARE. I'll be here t'morra.

MARY *goes out right.*

What should I have said?

*Silence.* CLARE *puts on his hat. He goes out left.*


SCENE THREE

*Littleport.*
*Road.*
*Night.*

BOB *and* MILES *carry* LAWRENCE *in.* LAWRENCE *is crying.*

BOB. The bushes.
PETER (*off*). Miles. Miles.
MILES (*shouting back*). Lawrence is hurt.
BOB (*to* LAWRENCE). Git crep in they bushes boy.
MILES. His row! They'll hear!

PETER *and* CLARE *come on.*

PETER. Who?
MILES. Lawrence. Cut 'bout the head. (*To* LAWRENCE.) Howd your row boy. You on't die.
PETER. We'll doo all the big houses. (*Blows his horn.*)
MILES. Ijit! (*To* CLARE.) See that gall from Milton's house?
CLARE. Mary?
MILES. That what they call her? Gall up there last winter.
CLARE. You see her?
MILES (*indicating*). Runnin' across them fields.
PETER. Mr Wicken – screw a pound out a him.

CLARE *hurries out.*

BOB. Then Mrs Hadchit's.
MILES. No, her first. She on't no bother. Wicken! – that cantankerous bastard'll need workin' over.

BOB (*to* LAWRENCE). Howd on boy. We'll be back.
CLARE (*off*). Mary!

PETER, BOB *and* MILES *start to go.*

BOB. Then parson!
PETER. ⎱
MILES. ⎰ Ay parson!
PETER. Thass the laddo. (*Blows horn.*)

DARKIE *and* HAMO *come in.*

DARKIE. Whole village up t'night!

BETTY *comes in from the opposite direction. She is laughing.
She carries a sheet.*

BETTY. Silver. Look. (*She shows them three candlesticks.*)
MILES. Mrs Hadchit's next.

PETER, BOB *and* MILES *go out.*

HAMO. Git hung takin' property.
DARKIE. Don't talk so far back boy! (*To* BETTY.) Keep 'em out a
sight. Give 'em t'the carter when thass all over. He'll sell 'em
up London.
BETTY. Proper silver. (*Looks at her reflection.*) See yourself in the
side, twist up. On't need candles in 'em. Light the room up by
themselves.
HAMO. Put them away, gall. Scare me.
BETTY. Mrs Hadchit's. Git inside her cupboards!
HAMO (*going.*). There on't be nothin' left.

BETTY *is hiding the candlesticks in the bushes. She screams.*

HAMO. ⎱ What?
DARKIE. ⎰ Soldiers?
BETTY. Dead man.
DARKIE. The bushes!
LAWRENCE. Betty I'm alive.
BETTY. Oh god it's young Lawrence Star. Whatever's happen,
Lawrence?
LAWRENCE. My head's cut about.

DARKIE. Tie him up, gall.

BETTY. Should us git a doctor?

DARKIE. They'd hand him over.

BETTY. My linen off Farmer Fab's. Gooin' a dye that an' run up a skirt. On't tell where it's come from then. Smart clean stuff. (*Binds* LAWRENCE's *head in the sheet.*) Shame! . . . Never had nothin' like that afore an' I on't had that ten minutes. Well that'll keep the blood in. Hurt on't harm. You keep an eye on my candlesticks. Anyone come sit up an' goo like a ghost. They'll soon run. I got 'em first: they're mine.

MILES *comes on.*

MILES. Darkie! Darkie! Darkie!

DARKIE. What's that, boy?

MILES. On't you come t'parsons?

MARY *comes on.*

MARY. All the big houses. The Mill. Old Mrs Shaft's the harlot. Straight up the front gate an' pick the roses –

BETTY. An' cabbage.

MARY. On't allowed in afore 'cept t'work. Tap front door. Say the poor's collectin'. Git off they say! Break the winders. Howd out your apron. Where's the silver under your floor? No silver here! Tap their heads with a stick. See the silver then. Jump out their pockets! Gold teeth out their heads! Tap tap. We'll be rich t'night. (*Stops.*) I smell silver!

BETTY. Silver on't smell.

MARY. Red pumice powder. Clean silver every day in Lord Milton's house. Know that smell. Money lender's guts!

MARY *goes into the bushes.*

BETTY. Leave that gall!

MARY (*finds candlesticks*). Silver. Knew t'was. On't touch your stuff gall. But you tie 'em on the end a rope an' drop 'em in the river out a my reach.

DARKIE, MILES *and* HAMO *laugh.*

Come on. Parson's.

MARY *goes out.*

MILES. I'll knock the landlord up the Globe. Thirsty work!

BETTY. Nose on her like an animal. On't hide 'em in the river for her t'goo fishin'. Bury 'em.

MILES *goes out right. The others go out left.* LAWRENCE *is alone.*

HAMO (*off*). Split both ways lads case he bolt. You goo the lanes. We'll cut across the fields.

*Off, the distant sound of the horn. The* GENTLEMEN *come in.*

FIRST GENTLEMAN. Listen. Children.

THIRD GENTLEMAN. We'll cut them off before they reach the parsonage.

FIRST GENTLEMAN. No – don't meddle. Wait for Milton.

THIRD GENTLEMAN. What? If we let them get the bit between their teeth –

FIRST GENTLEMAN. What can they do? Enough damage to bring them to Assizes. This has been coming on long enough. Strangers creeping over fields, burning ricks, breaking machines, laming cattle – and vanishing. No one's seen them. No one knows anything. Well after tonight we'll have names.

SECOND GENTLEMAN. Yes. We'll watch from a safe distance.

THIRD GENTLEMAN. If they come on my land I shoot.

*The* GENTLEMEN *go out.* LAWRENCE *sits up. His head is wrapped in the sheet. It seems an enormous bundle. He starts to cry.*

LAWRENCE (*crawling*). Hev t'goo ... (*Tries to stand. Falls. Lies and cries.*) O god ...

MILES *comes on with some bottles. He looks round for* LAWRENCE.

MILES. Lawrence? (*Sees him.*) Where you gooin' boy?

LAWRENCE. Gen'men. We'll git hang Miles.

MILES. How many?

LAWRENCE. Gen'men. Tell from their voices.

MILES. How many?

CLARE *comes on.*

CLARE. I can't find her Miles!

MILES. On't time goo chasin' galls. Gen'men here. Lawrence?

LAWRENCE. My head. That on't stop bleedin'.

CLARE. Which way she goo?

MILES (*to* LAWRENCE). Drink some a this boy.

CLARE (*calls*). Mary! – Hev she say anythin'? Were she lookin' for me?

LAWRENCE *drinks from the bottle.*

MILES. Hev they talk a soldiers boy? Think!

LAWRENCE. Blood run down my ears.

CLARE (*going*). Mary! Mary! Mary!

CLARE *goes out.*

MILES. Git back under that hedge. (*Helps* LAWRENCE *into the hedge.*) I'll git the others. Pick you up on the way back. (*Off, the horn sounds in the far distance.*) Damn ijit row!

MILES *goes out.* LAWRENCE *starts to crawl again.*

LAWRENCE (*crying*). Miles . . . They'll hang us . . . Hev t'goo . . .

PARSON *comes in. He is out of breath.*

PARSON. O dear dear. (*Stands still. Looks round.*) The moon will come out. O dear dear dear.

LAWRENCE *starts to cry. He tries to stop it.*

Who's that? Who's laughing at me? (*Whimpering.*) Cowards! Hunting an old man! O god how many?

PARSON *tries to hide in the hedge and quieten his breathing.*

Who's there? Lord Milton's men? Don't shoot. (*Stands.*) What is . . .? A little boy crying? I'm not used to being out without a lantern. Stop it? (*He trips over* LAWRENCE.) Ah! – bottles. How foolish and disgusting. Lying there in beer and your own blood. Will you find peace in a bottle? Stop crying boy. God knows who'll hear – your people or mine. Are you badly cut? Not if you can still cry.

*The* PARSON *sits on a tree stump.*

Lord Milton's men will get you to a doctor – *your* people can't help you now. Stop it! (*Slight pause.*) And after this terrible night? – when I ride down a lane and meet a labourer can we look each other in the face? I baptized him and we can't give each other a decent good morning. They'll raise their hats like an insult. O try to stop crying! The whole system will go out of their lives. We'll be reduced to relying on anger or strength or our wits – master *and* servant. And then what are we? – animals trying to live in houses. For one night's violence and a handful of silver to spend on drink!

DARKIE, MILES *and* BOB *come in.*

DARKIE. If I believed your lies I'd say we were meant to meet· Left your place an' was off home – an' there you are stood cross our way.

PARSON. Your friend. See to him. He can't stop crying. Some nervous reaction.

BOB. We're collecting.

MILES. From rich farmers, shopkeepers –

BETTY *comes in.*

BOB. He farm.

DARKIE. Spend more time writin' pigs in his book than readin' the Bible.

PARSON. I have nothing on me.

DARKIE. Shall us escort you back t'parson's?

PARSON. I shall not give way to violence –

DARKIE. Turn your pockets out.

PARSON. – and go against every principle I've lived by. How could I call you my flock if I betrayed the good shepherd's laws – from cowardice?

BOB. Git up.

PARSON (*not moving*). An old man powerless before you. I do not want to think I've blessed savages from my altar –

MARY *and* PETER *come in. They all stand some way from the* PARSON.

MILES. Show us your pockets!

DARKIE (*goes to the* PARSON, *jerks him to his feet and searches his pockets. The others begin to move in closer to the* PARSON). Silver in this pocket. Notebook in a silver case. Corn prices in that. Silver pencil. Gold ring. (*Pulls it from the* PARSON's *finger.*) Cross on chain. Gold. (*Yanks chain free.*) Silver knob end his stick. (*Snaps the walking stick over his leg and throws the knob to the others.*)

BETTY. They buttons! Pearly buttons!

MARY. Fasten them on the back with a gold stud. Show you how thass done.

> MARY *and* BETTY *start to take off the* PARSON's *buttons.* LAWRENCE *crawls slowly out of the hedge. He tries to drag himself away. He is weaker. He cries. The sheet is soaked in blood.*

PARSON. Aren't you ashamed?

BETTY. No. No. No. No. I on't ashamed. I'm ashamed I can't feed my kid.

MARY (*working at buttons. Laughs*). Let me. Thass it.

PETER. I'm ashamed I work in parson's field an' crawl home like an animal.

MILES. I'm ashamed the sweat roll off me while you git fat!

MARY (*laughing*). Thass five.

HAMO. I'm ashamed t'goo t'sleep with the dirt out your fields on me hands every night.

MARY (*searching the ground*). Drop one.

PARSON. I'm an old man –

> PETER *blows his horn.*

MILES. Git his collar!

MARY (*searching on the ground*). Irish linen!

BOB. Git his shoes!

HAMO. You on't wear leather like that.

PARSON. People of my parish. Stripping an old man –

BETTY (*touching the shoes*). Softer'n gloves.

MARY (*searching on the ground*). Mind that stud. (*Picks it up.*)

DARKIE. Git his coat. Git it off.

PARSON. O god look down and judge –

MILES. Under that he's same as us.

DARKIE. You cold now?

PETER. Take his shirt.

BETTY. Git it off.

BOB. Off.

HAMO. Off.

BETTY. Pull it off.

MARY. Mind that tear!

BETTY. I'll hev it.

MILES. Pull it off.

DARKIE. Your flesh cold now boy? 'Fraid I put my fist in your face? Hev a fist in my face all day. On't like my fist wave in your eye? Hev a fist stuck in my eye every day.

BOB. More clothes under that.

BETTY. Walkin' shop!

> PETER *blows his horn.*

MILES. Vest off.

HAMO. Git that off.

BOB. Let's see his flesh.

BETTY. Off. Off.

PETER. Off.

> *The* PARSON *stands stripped. His long grey hair falls over his face. He shivers. They stare at him for a moment.* LAWRENCE *still crawls slowly over the stage.*

BOB (*child-like innocence*) . . . How they wash an' care for that!

MARY. Let's goo. Thass all he's got. Gen'men about.

> MARY *picks up shoes, clothes and bottles. She runs out while they talk.*

BETTY. My baby. My baby on't got proper baby skin like that. Look how soft that is. Like silk lace. My baby's born hard – hev animal skin like summat live in the road. (*Pinches the* PARSON's *flesh.*) Look at that. Come away in handfuls.

MILES. Look! Handful a flesh!

HAMO. Handfuls!

PARSON (*yells as they grab his skin*). Ah! Ah!

DARKIE. Our flesh. That belong t'us. Where you took that flesh boy? You took that flesh off her baby. My ma. They on't got proper flesh on em now.

*They pull at his skin.*

BETTY. My flesh.

BOB. Her baby's flesh.

PETER. Our flesh.

DARKIE. Where you stole that flesh boy? Your flesh is stolen goods. You're covered in stolen goods when you strip! How you climb your altar steps like that? What god say when you raise Chriss flesh in service? – more flesh they stolen doo he say? You call us thief when we took silver. You took us flesh!

BETTY *cries.* LAWRENCE *stops crawling. The sheet has unwound from his head and dragged over the ground. He lies and cries.*

BETTY. My baby. My baby.

*The others cry. The* PARSON *weeps and mumbles prayers.*

DARKIE (*in tears*). When you laugh you use our voice. When you goo straight you took us backs. Thass why we're bent.

MILES (*in tears*). O god o god how shall us ever git our things back. All the things they stolen.

BOB (*in tears*). What shall us ever do?

PARSON. God of the merciful . . . father of heaven . . . (*He stops.*)

DARKIE. Nothin' t'say? He hev the truth now. More truth than all the bishops an' lords'll tell him. An' he say nothin'. Ay well: we said the truth t'night an' he can't answer.

BETTY (*crying quietly*). Baby. Baby.

MILES. The truth.

HAMO. Ay.

BETTY (*throws* LAWRENCE's *blood-stained linen at the* PARSON). Cover yourself. (PARSON *doesn't move. Angrily.*) Cover it! On't you throw charity back in my face!

*The* PARSON *covers himself with the linen.*

You stood there two minute boy. I'm made a mock of all my

life. (*Quietly again, she holds a button up between her thumb and index finger.*) Yes, yes. Look at the buttons t'cover his thievin.' An' my little un on't never git a morsel she on't cried for. He'll bury her, will he feed her?

LAWRENCE *crawls back into the bushes.*

DARKIE. You lay charge against us or give evidence?

PARSON. The cross is always humiliated. What have I suffered? A little humiliation and cold. I shall stand to the truth. I cannot betray the life I've lived till now. How could I go on living? From now on my thoughts shall only be of death.

BETTY (*to* PARSON). Hush your row boy. You on't a child. Don't talk so scandalous – an' you hush Lawrence.

MILTON *comes on with the three* GENTLEMEN.

MILTON. Give Mr Twice your coat.

THIRD GENTLEMAN (*covering* PARSON *with his coat*). A mob destroying in a minute the work of centuries –

MILTON (*calmly*). Quiet.

THIRD GENTLEMAN. – broken windows, old folk in tears, looting –

MILTON (*calmly but decisively*). Be quiet. Mr Twice stay the night at my house. I sent your family and servants on ahead. Mr Harvington will take you to the house.

PARSON (*looking at his bare feet*). My lord, my feet . . .

MILTON. Mr Harvington will carry you.

THIRD GENTLEMAN *picks the* PARSON *up.*

PARSON. Thank you.

THIRD GENTLEMAN *carries the* PARSON *out.*

MILTON. These gentlemen are special constables. I swore them in tonight. I was called away from dinner – and I find you misbehaving like children. Go home. Let us avoid any more violence.

DARKIE. You steal from us. Parson steal from us. What we doo t'parson? Make a mock. Took – what? Trinkets! When I steal

from parson what you doo t'me? Law hang us. Thass the on'y
difference 'tween you an' me: you on't think twice 'fore you use
violence.

MILTON. Take your cap off.

MILES. Don't. He want you recognized.

> *A shot.* LAWRENCE *yells and dies. The* GENTLEMEN *aim
> their guns.*

MILTON. Stop!

BETTY. Lawrence! (*Starts to go to him.*)

MILTON. Stop! (BETTY *stops. To* SECOND GENTLEMAN.) Go
and look.

> SECOND GENTLEMAN *goes to the body.* BETTY *cries.*

MILES. Bastards.

DARKIE. He's dead.

SECOND GENTLEMAN (*looking up*). I'm afraid my bullet went
through his temple.

MILTON (*orders*). Bind his head. That sheet. You and you – carry
him to the horses. All of you march behind. You'll be covered
with the guns. (*To* SECOND GENTLEMAN.) Yes?

SECOND GENTLEMAN. Sir.

> MILES *and* HAMO *carry* LAWRENCE *out. The two of them
> cry quietly.* LAWRENCE'*s head is wrapped in the sheet.*

MILTON. Follow them.

> *The rest go out.*


## SCENE FOUR

*Ely.*
*Cell.*
*Evening.*

*Quiet. Dark. Pale light from two small high grated windows. Bench.
Blankets.*

DARKIE, MILES, BOB *and* HAMO *looking towards the door as it opens.* WARDER *comes in. He gives each man a bowl of soup and a lump of bread.*

WARDER (*to* DARKIE, *as he gives the food out*). Your mates outside on a visit.

WARDER *goes out.*

BOB. On't touch it.

MILES. Eat. Sorry you starved when they let you out.

BOB *eats. The door opens.* PATTY *and* CLARE *come in in travelling clothes. The door is shut behind them.* PATTY *carries a jacket.*

PATTY (*puts her arms round* DARKIE). O dear my boy.
BOB, MILES. } 'Lo gall.
HAMO.
PATTY. My dears. All.
CLARE. On't let us interrupt your grub.

*They eat while they talk.*

DARKIE. All right at home? (PATTY *shakes her head.*) Ma?
PATTY (*nods*). Took t'bed. On't git up. Lie by winder. I on't know. (*Silence.*) Say I hev t'bring your good jacket. On't goo like a tramp an' disgrace the family.

PATTY *cries for a few seconds. They eat.*

DARKIE. Quiet pal?

CLARE *smiles and nods.*

BOB. Never thought it'd come t'this. Thing like this . . .

*Silence.*

DARKIE. Mum ill then?
PATTY. Git old.
DARKIE. Lot a talk outside?
PATTY. Ely's full a army.

HAMO. Say bishop'll give a sermon. All judges goo in cathedral arm in arm. Proper sight.

MILES. Bishop like t'fix the rope his-self. On'y way he git satisfaction. Great hog. Twenty four. No they on't goo through with it. What people say?

PATTY. On't rightly tell. Stand on street corners like the whole week's market. On't understand n'more.

MILES. On't they say –

PATTY (*irritated*). How'd I know *what* they say? (*Silence. She collects the bowls and stacks them neatly by the door before she speaks.*) O boy *I* don't know what t' say. Thass a fact. (*Trying not to cry.*) Allus a good boy Darkie. Stood up for the right. On't hurt a fly out askin' pardon. All a you. They on't know.

MILES. An' you can't tell em.

DARKIE. On't goo through with it. Ship us off t'Australia. (*To* CLARE.) Lucky you dodged off before the law got us.

PATTY. He's had another drop a luck – so p'raps your's'll change.

DARKIE. What's that?

PATTY. Scribblin' come t'summat. Gen'man bin. Talk 'bout a book.

DARKIE. O.

PATTY. Says he'll travel. If that goo well. London.

DARKIE (*after a pause*). Who's that?

PATTY. You on't know. Gen'man.

MILES. What you git boy? Hev t'pay you summat.

CLARE *shrugs.*

DARKIE. No thass good John. On't be ashamed a that.

MILES. What you write boy? Write 'bout this place. What goo on.

CLARE. Who'd read that?

PATTY (*pride*). Gen'man come though on't he boy? (*Silence.*) Well thass a long way gettin' here but I'm glad I made the effort. Hev t'goo soon Darkie. Git a start fore it's dark. Any errands? Miles?

MILES. No, gall.

*Silence.* CLARE *starts to laugh. He tries to stop.*

PATTY. John. What's up boy?

CLARE. On't – (*He stops laughing but starts again.*) – nothin' –

DARKIE (*smiles*). Thass right. On't goo through with it.

BOB (*giggling*). Twenty four.

DARKIE (*laughing slightly*). On't allow. Government stop it.

MILES (*to* CLARE, *a bit frightened but grinning*). What you laugh at boy?

PATTY (*giggling with embarrassment*). Behave John an' give over. (*She folds the jacket on her lap and pats it.*) Look good when you're all dress up Darkie. Stickler for being clean.

> PARSON *comes in. They stop laughing.*

PARSON. I was visiting the others and I thought ... May I? (*He comes into the room. He shuts the door.*) I have not come to offer hope. If you don't die at the end of the week you will all die in time. To those outside this prison that would sound like cant. But you inside can understand it now. When you stripped me in the forest I stood with naked feet on the earth that will be my grave. I heard the devils laugh at my sins. I saw myself judged and condemned – as we all are. If not tomorrow then soon. (PATTY *makes an awkward gesture with the coat.*) Do you understand that my dear?

PATTY (*confused*). Just visitin' sir. Brought my brother's new coat. Believe in church though.

PARSON. How small and impotent we are. We clear a few fields, build a few houses, twist a few rods of iron, and think our laws are everlasting. But the world is the Lord's for he rules time. Forget this world, its misery and waste, all luxury and vice, its painted vanities. Think only of the brightness of god. Rejoice! His mercy welcomes. His joy is to forgive. Do you understand at last? (*Slight silence. He begins to plead.*) Die to this dark world. Live in eternal day. (BOB *cries a little. The* PARSON *turns to him eagerly. He takes the crying as a sign.*) Yes, yes. (*Quietly.*) God is here. God enters through these bars. Reach out. Touch his garments.

> WARDER *comes in.*

WARDER. Step outside sir.

PARSON. This is not –
WARDER. Governor says outside.

*PARSON and* WARDER *go out.* WARDER *shuts the door behind them.*

MILES. On't a scratch on him.

*Outside a woman's laugh spirals up inside the prison. Another woman joins in. A group of people laugh.*

MILES (*looks at* CLARE). You got 'em all gooin' boy.

*The laughter fades out. Then a man laughs closer and the group laugh again. Everyone in the cell stands.*

DARKIE. Lettin' us off.
BOB. Listen.
HAMO. Why on't they come here?
BOB. Hev they goo pass?
HAMO. On't they let us off?
DARKIE. Quiet! Other rooms first.

MILES *listens at the door. Everyone in the cell is silent. The laughter goes on.*

MILES (*calling*). Shut up! (*To others.*) Laugh too loud. On't hear.
DARKIE (*to* CLARE). Goo out boy. They'll let you out.
BOB (*banging on the door*). Here! Here! Here! Here!
DARKIE (*to* BOB). Shut up, boy!

HAMO, BOB *and* PATTY *beat on the door and shout.*

HAMO. ⎫
BOB. ⎬ Here! Here! Here! Here!
PATTY. Let's out! Let's out! On't a prisoner!

*Outside the laughter goes on and on. Screams, shouts, peals, groans – of laughter. No one laughs in the room. Their hysteria is dry. They stop banging. They move away from the door. They go to the other side of the room. They stare at the door. They huddle together. The door opens.* GOVERNOR, WARDER *and* PARSON *come in.* WARDER *gives* BOB *a thumbs up sign.*

GOVERNOR. I have received a document from London. Listen carefully. Noise Hicks.

WARDER *goes out through the door. He leaves it open.*

After studying the proceedings of the special assize that last week –

WARDER (*off*). Howd your row!

GOVERNOR – sentenced you to hang –

*The* WARDER *comes in. The laughter goes on.*

– the authorities have provided me with a list –

WARDER. I told 'em.

GOVERNOR. – of condemned whose sentences have been commuted to such alternative punishments –

PATTY. I knew they had t'let yoo off! On't git coffins in this town. Local shops on't provide. Know what'd happen t'their winders. Had t'send all the way t'Cambridge. On't even git the loan of a cart t' –

GOVERNOR (*talking her down*) – as London deems appropriate. I have still to be informed of these. (*Reads list.*) Miles Cooper.

MILES. Sir.

GOVERNOR. Hamish Cecil Towsey.

HAMO. Sir.

GOVERNOR. Peter Star –

WARDER. Last room sir.

GOVERNOR. Robert Hall.

BOB. O bless 'em. Bless 'em –

GOVERNOR. That is the list for this room.

HAMO. Thanks be t'god.

MILES. Bless 'em. Bless 'em.

PARSON. You men vow now! O vow! Remember this moment. God took you to the graveside –

GOVERNOR. Last room.

PARSON. – and you saw its shadow. O take –

BOB. Bless 'em.

PARSON. – that shadow and let it be the mirror for your minds.

GOVERNOR *and* WARDER *have gone out.* PARSON *turns to* DARKIE.

They will die of typhus in the galleys. Drown. Spend their lives in prison. And they laugh!

*Laughter goes round the prison. Everyone in the room except* DARKIE *and* PARSON *laugh with nervous hysteria.*

They'll never see the place where they were born. Wives and children will vanish from their lives. Listen to them laugh!

*A closer burst of laughter from the next room.*

Their world will be so strange they won't know their face in the glass or the world outside the window. They'll dig rocks to plant seed. When they die they'll be buried in shallow graves – men will have long since forgotten the customs for the dead. Listen! (*Laughter.*) Abandon this bitter hope. Hope! – it is a tide that goes in and out and grinds men together till they wear each other down. Take your scaffold from god's hand. He crushes a life's despair into a few seconds. I will walk with you to the scaffold. I'll have a word with the prison ordinary about it.

*The* PARSON *hurries out.*

DARKIE (*to* CLARE). Take my coat. Here boy. On't just show, was it Patty. Good strong stuff. Work hard t'wear that out.
MILES (*involuntary happiness*). O god.
BOB. Saved! On't he said?
HAMO. Must be true. They're laughin'.
DARKIE. Goo on, take it. On't waste it on show. Kep' us in rags, on't dress up for 'em when I die. On't their circus.

CLARE *takes the coat.*

On't – feel straight in my head. I'll be a bit quiet.

*The door opens.* BETTY *runs in.*

BETTY. O boys hev you all bin saved! (*Laughs and embraces the prisoners.*) Boy. Boy. Bob my lad.
BOB. Bless 'em. Bless 'em.

WARDER *comes in.*

WARDER. Git out gall! What you think this is? Cooper, Towsey, Hall: things t'gither an' git next door.

MILES. I'll stay with him.

WARDER. Next door.

MILES. On't right. (*To* DARKIE.) Let us off t'be harder on you.

DARKIE. Bob on't more'n a lad. You got your wife and kids. Best me if it had t'be someone.

WARDER. Move sharp.

> MILES, HAMO *and* BOB *collect their things.* BETTY *helps.*

CLARE. Look at the fly gooin' in an' out the bars. You could climb up an kill it but you on't. Patty stay in town t'night. Likely they'll let you lie out in the corridor. I'll come again t'morra.

GOVERNOR (*off*). I ordered quiet!

PATTY (*unsure*). Darkie.

DARKIE. No need t' stay in this place. On'y git upset.

> *The prison goes quiet.*

PATTY. Stay if you ask.

DARKIE. On't want it.

> MILES, HAMO, BOB *and* BETTY *go out.*

BETTY (*outside the door*). On't Darkie saved then?

WARDER (*in the doorway*). Five left t'hang.

> *The* WARDER *goes out and shuts the door.* CLARE *sits on the bench with his head in his hands.* DARKIE *and* PATTY *stand.* CLARE *begins to laugh. It is easy, not hysterical, but not calm. It wells up in him and overflows.*

PATTY. Stop it. Shameful.

CLARE (*laughing into his hands*). Can't.

PATTY. Stop it. Doo I goo back on me own.

> CLARE *lies on the bench. He covers himself with the blanket to muffle the sound.*

Allus find some carry on! Wicked!

CLARE *falls on the floor. He rolls about under the blanket. Off, there is a short burst of laughter. It becomes hysterical – like sobbing. It lasts for a few seconds.* CLARE *laughs happily through it.*

CLARE. Hurts. Hurts.

WARDER *comes in. He watches from the doorway.*

WARDER (*nods at* DARKIE). Thought you'd gone off your head. Happens sometime.

PATTY (*giggling politely*). Is he hurt? On't right. Ought a think a Darkie. Not allus self. (*Hands over ears.*) Stop it Mr Clare.

WARDER *comes into the room.*

My head goo. (*Screams*). Stop it!

PARSON *appears in the doorway.*

PARSON. Keep that man quiet. This house has seen enough levity.

PARSON *goes.*

WARDER. Howd your racket.

DARKIE. Let him be. Bad seth t'him, why should I stop him?

WARDER (*to* DARKIE). Stay civil! (*Gestures after* PARSON.) Parson'll rattle t'Governor an' I'll git it in the neck. On't make trouble for me boy, doo I'll make trouble for you! (*Pulls the blanket off* CLARE.) Drunk. Pair a you git off.

WARDER *goes to the door and waits.* CLARE *stops laughing.*

DARKIE. Best mate I had John. Keep your luck. On't fit in at home. Sorry mother's upset but thass a bit late. Well I on't the son she'd hev chose. Look arter my sister. (*To* PATTY.) On't come. Rather you on't. (*No answer.*) Expect you'll doo what you think best.

PATTY. On't ought a said you on't fit in. No cause t'burden us with that. You on't know.

DARKIE. Can't say the right things in this place.

PATTY *goes out.*

CLARE. Had a gall with you that night. Gall worked at Milton's.
DARKIE. What?
CLARE. You on't know her name. Saw her last Christmas.

*Off, a short burst of laughter.*

DARKIE. What you up to boy?
CLARE. Hev she told you where she were gooin'?
DARKIE (*shrugs*). All that row. Some got away.
CLARE. But on't she said –
DARKIE. Chriss sake boy! (*Slight pause.*) Patty's stood outside.
CLARE (*after a pause*). On't quarrel Darkie.
DARKIE. No.

WARDER *stands aside.* CLARE *goes out.*


# SCENE FIVE

*Hyde Park.*
*Day.*

CLARE *downstage with* MRS EMMERSON. *He wears* DARKIE'S *green jacket. She is about forty.*

*Upstage a prize fight.* PORTER, *a negro, and* JACKSON, *an Irishman, are stripped to the waist, wear tights, and fight with bare knuckles. A tubby referee. Backers.* PORTER'S *backers are:* FIRST *a marquis, and* SECOND *the marquis's fellow Harrow school friend.* JACKSON'S *backers are:* THIRD *the young son of a shopkeeper, and* FOURTH *a greasy old cockney. The* BACKERS' *jackets on the ground mark the ring.*

MRS EMMERSON. The admiral said we should meet him here on his afternoon walk. You are nervous, Mr Clare.
CLARE. Ay.
MRS EMMERSON. No need. He subscribed for twelve copies of your book. Such a subscriber attracts interest.
CLARE. Ay.

### The Fight

*The* FIGHTERS *are fresh. They move lightly on their toes.*

FIRST BACKER. Watch the fella Porter.
SECOND BACKER. Ware the fella's left.
FIRST BACKER. You're not here to bow to each other.
THIRD BACKER. After him Jackson. Get stuck into him.
FOURTH BACKER. Nicely Jackie boy.
REFEREE. Corners Gents.

*End of Round One*

MRS EMMERSON. See, Mr Clare, we have grass and trees in this park. Do they not inspire you? O to be touched by the wings! The rushing of the spirit! We earthly ones can but crane our necks to watch you soar! Mr Clare, shall I slip into yonder hedge and leave you to the muse?
CLARE. Tell-'e-true mam I'd like t'be alone with my thoughts – so long as you on't goo too far.
REFEREE. Right lads.

*Start of Round Two*

MRS EMMERSON. But wait! I promised Patty to stay at your side in the great city. I underlined it in my letter.
CLARE. You could kip an eye on me from the bushes mam.
MRS EMMERSON. O Mr Clare, I could hardly come upon the admiral from the bushes – even in the company of a poet. (*Laughs.*) I will tell the truth. (*Showing.*) Notebook and pencil. It is my ambition to be at your side when the muse calls. I shall take down your words as you cast them on the air. When I'm old with my nieces and nephews gathered at my skirts I shall take out this book and turn – commanded by their childish piping: it will be their habitual pleasure! – to the oft op't pages where I wrote the effusions of John Clare. 'Hyde Park Impromptu'. Now comes tom-sparrow on his feathered wing, the city bird that cannot sing, but ah I know within thy heart, what thoughts are longing to –. The last line is often difficult to bring home.
CLARE. It flew. Like the sparrer.

MRS EMMERSON. Mr Clare, my silly chatter! Well, I've done you some good and I shall do more.

## The Fight

FIRST BACKER. That nicked the Irishman's smiling eye.
THIRD BACKER. Use the left. Jab. Jab.
FOURTH BACKER. Nicely Jackie boy.
SECOND BACKER. Hack at him Porter. Up the blackman.
FIRST BACKER. Left jab then tap the solar plexus.
REFEREE. Corners gents.

*End of Round Two.*

MRS EMMERSON. This is a popular refuge for poets. Away from the hot London streets. The air should be filled with music. I call it poets' corner. Though happily the poets are living. Who's that? My eyes in this bright light. I read too much.
CLARE. Lamb.
MRS EMMERSON. Have they told you about Lamb?
CLARE. They all have.
MRS EMMERSON. His sister killed his mother with the bread knife. They put her away – but Lamb promised to stay with her all the time and they let her out. Poor lamb! The insane live so long. No money – he works as a clerk. He can't support his sister *and* marry – so he drinks. They carry her strait-jacket everywhere. In the ornamental bag.

## The Fight

REFEREE. Right gents.

*Round Three starts. There is a quick knockdown.*

REFEREE. Right gents.

*End of Round Three.*

FIRST BACKER. Watch his left Porter. Beat you twice. Watch his feet. Irish go in for dancing.
SECOND BACKER. Chip him down.
THIRD BACKER (*to* JACKSON *as he breathes*). Deeper.

FOURTH BACKER. In out. In out.

> CHARLES *and* MARY LAMB *come in.* CHARLES *is young, lean, handsome and dressed as a literary romantic.* MARY *is ten years older than* CHARLES. *She wears a respectable hat and carries the ornamental bag.* LAMB *hesitates when he sees* MRS EMMERSON *but comes forward.*

LAMB. John.

CLARE. Respects brother.

LAMB (*to* MRS EMMERSON). Mam. John, my sister, Mary.

CLARE. Mary had a little lamb. Is that knowed up in London? Everywhere that Mary went the Lamb was sure to goo! (*Laughs.*)

MRS EMMERSON. Hyde Park reminds Clare of his native country. We almost had a poem on it, did we not?

LAMB. Now you've seen us will you desert your village?

MRS EMMERSON. No, John will go back to his wife and cottage. We are agreed.

LAMB. Are *you* agreed brother Clare?

CLARE. Ay. On't afford London.

> LAMB *and* MRS EMMERSON *laugh.*

LAMB. None of us can afford London. Well you're a wise poet. Stay at home where the muse has your address.

### The Fight

REFEREE. Gents.

*Round Four starts*

THIRD BACKER. Move the big clumsy bear.

FIRST BACKER. Let him do his jig Porter. And make him wince so he's got music to do it to.

SECOND BACKER. Fella'll soon lose his puff.

FIRST BACKER. Then you can bend him over your knee and break his back a vertebra at a time.

REFEREE. Part lads.

*End of Round Four.*

MARY LAMB. The shopping Charles.

LAMB. And my office.

SECOND BACKER. The marquis will see you all right Porter. He's a good judge of flesh. The light in his eye means money.

THIRD BACKER. Move him.

LAMB. I wanted to tell you in the crush last night: I like your verse.

MRS EMMERSON. There'll be another book soon – if our plans prosper.

LAMB. Clare tells the truth.

MRS EMMERSON. What is the truth?

LAMB. Pilate asked Christ that but he didn't wait for an answer. If he had he would have crucified it.

MRS EMMERSON (*uncertain*). Tut tut, Mr Lamb. Is that not free thought?

LAMB. Mrs Emmerson you are the only person who's ever really said tut tut.

MRS EMMERSON. O fie!

LAMB. Truth isn't governed by the laws of supply and demand. When it's scarce its price goes down. So it's not a luxury, it's never found in palaces, or paraded by judges. Truth shelters in the gutter. Only the man who stoops finds it.

MRS EMMERSON. I'm proud to say I didn't understand one word. Mr Lamb, you are a poet. You have no call to go round putting ideas in people's heads.

LAMB. Even the hangman tells the truth when he's drunk. Keats went to Rome to find truth – and beauty and life. He died there. Truth is often ugly. The spit on god's face. Yes, the truth is spat into the golden faces of all idols. God's face is covered in spit. Fools think that's his mask and worship it. Dangerous! But it's even more dangerous when the truth is told by a wise man. The goddess of wisdom is a bird of prey, the owl. But the fools have hunted *her* and put her in a cage. If you try to let her out she savages your hand. Only a wise man tries to do that – or another sort of fool.

*He comes downstage and turns his back on the others.*

That was the lunchtime sermon. Now the blessing. (*He takes out his flask.*) To truth. (*He shakes it.*) In vino veritas.

### The Fight

REFEREE. Right gents.

*Round Five starts.*

SECOND BACKER. Go for the cut on the fella's eye.
FIRST BACKER. Stretch the cut.
THIRD BACKER. Use your science.
SECOND BACKER. He thinks science is the English shillalah.
FIRST BACKER. Keep your fist in his face Porter.
MARY LAMB. In this hot weather the vegetables are covered in dust. It's as oily as soot. The water goes black when you wash them. They're going off before you get them home. I complain to the shopkeepers –

> LAMB *sees they are listening to her, drinks from his flask and crosses himself.*

– but they say they have to display their goods. They soon complain if you touch them or smell them. Goods? – I tell them they should call them bads.

> *She laughs. She takes a cabbage from the ornamental bag.*

I bought this cabbage yesterday. It smells of fish.

> *She smells it and puts it under* MRS EMMERSON's *nose.*

Mackerel or sprats?

MRS EMMERSON. I have no sense of smell.
LAMB. I write on the back of bills and promissory notes when the Governor's out of the office.
MRS EMMERSON. John doesn't know what they are.
CLARE (*smiles excitedly*). Ay. Bills are never paid and promises never kept.

### The Fight

FIRST BACKER. Play the fella Porter.
FOURTH BACKER. Ouch.

SECOND BACKER *laughs.*

THIRD BACKER. Lout! Use your feet if you can't use your head!
SECOND BACKER. He's yours now! Ouch!

*ADMIRAL RADSTOCK comes in. Large, dignified, grey-haired.
He watches the fight. The others do not see him at first.*

**The Fight**

REFEREE. Right lads.

*End of Round Five.*

THIRD BACKER. Dam' it you give him your eye to carve up!
FIRST BACKER. He'll come like a well trained puppy now and
stand to be whipped. Don't thrash him too soon. No better
pastime than watching a big punchy bruiser taking punish-
ment. Don't let the fella duck it by passing out.
SECOND BACKER. Bang him and keep him raw.
PORTER (*laughs*). I play him suh. Have my piece of fun and hurt
him real hard.
SECOND BACKER (*calls to the other corner*). Send him back to his
Irish bog.
FOURTH BACKER. Yer ain' won yet ol' sport.
THIRD BACKER. I invested in you Jackson. He's over confident.
You can stop that black ape. Just behave.
MRS EMMERSON. Lord Radstock, good day.
LAMB. Servant, sir.

MARY LAMB *bows.*

MRS EMMERSON. Allow me to present my friend. John Clare –
your benefactor.
CLARE. Servant sir.
ADMIRAL. Honoured, Mr Clare. Mrs Emmerson been rushing
you off your feet?
CLARE. Mrs Emmerson's bin most kind.
ADMIRAL (*after nodding approval*). Your verse. Great charm
there. True melody. Fine love of English landscape. (*Looks
at* LAMB.) Nothing mawkish – (*Turns back to* CLARE.) a

sailor or christian may read it with profit. I'm both. When I was away with the fleet I often had such thoughts. Couldn't put them on paper though. I'm glad now – with time on my hands – to be of use. How is Mr Emmerson?

MRS EMMERSON. As well as we may hope.

ADMIRAL. Ah.

### The Fight

REFEREE. Gentlemen then.

*Round Six starts.*

THIRD BACKER. Elbows. Head out the way.

SECOND BACKER. Punish him. Let him smart.

FOURTH BACKER. Ouch!

THIRD BACKER. Hit him! Hit him!

ADMIRAL. I have one reservation. Not serious. The fault of a narrow horizon. Those remarks in – poem named after your village –

MRS EMMERSON. Helpstone.

ADMIRAL. (You see we've discussed it) – which criticizes the landowning classes – smack of radicalism.

MRS EMMERSON (*reciting*). Accursed Wealth! –

ADMIRAL. That bit.

MRS EMMERSON. O'er bounding human laws
                    Of every evil then remainst the cause.

ADMIRAL. And so on.

MRS EMMERSON. Including lines from 'Winter'.
   (*Reciting.*)        What thousands now half pined and bare
                        Are forced to stand thy –
   (*Explains.*) That is, Winters –
   (*Reciting.*)                        – piercing air.

ADMIRAL. Now now, sir.

MRS EMMERSON. All day near numbed to death with cold
                    Some petty gentry –

ADMIRAL (*shaking his head*). At it again.

MRS EMMERSON.                        – to uphold.

ADMIRAL. Tut tut!

## The Fight

REFEREE. Corners gents.

*End of Round Six.*

FIRST BACKER. Put the fella down now Porter. Good sport but too much is damned sight worse than too little eh?

SECOND BACKER. Dinner wants orderin' properly.

FIRST BACKER (*slaps* PORTER's *shoulder*). Greek torso under that muck. If you could scrub it off you could stand on a pedestal.

PORTER. I'll do him this time suh.

THIRD BACKER. Keep out of his reach. You've only got to catch him once. He'll go down like an ox.

JACKSON. Ay ay.

FOURTH BANKER. Pecker up old lad.

REFEREE. Gents.

*Round Seven starts.*

THIRD BACKER. Remember Jackson. Let him thrash you and you're on the way down. No one else will back you. You make your own future.

FIRST BACKER. Do it stylish. It's worth a new suit.

ADMIRAL (*going to* CLARE). I shan't lecture you. Political science isn't parish pump philosophy. But answer this. Who controls the brute in man? Polite society. Well, your verse undermines its authority. There'd be chaos. The poor would be the first to suffer. I understand some hangings have already been necessary in your part of the world. Makes my point for me.

REFEREE. Corners gents.

*End of Round Seven.*

MRS EMMERSON. The admiral has a stateman's experience.

ADMIRAL. The people you criticize –

MRS EMMERSON. Unwittingly.

ADMIRAL. – are the only ones who can afford books. The only ones who can read! I ordered twelve. Now I can't give them to my friends. I can't tell you how to write verse. But I can spot a blemish. I'm a fellow author. Have you read my 'Cottager's

Friend, or a word in Season to him who is so Fortunate as to Possess a Bible or New Testament and a Book of Common Prayer'?

MRS EMMERSON. I gave John his copy.

ADMIRAL. In its twentieth edition. He should also look at my 'British Flag Triumphant'.

MRS EMMERSON (*writing*). I'll get it for him.

CLARE. The poems'd fall down.

ADMIRAL. Your publishers won't like you to alienate the already limited reading public and –

CLARE. On't see no nymphs in our fields but I seen a workhouse.

MRS EMMERSON. How does it help to shake your fist at heaven when some homeward-wending swain perishes in the snow?

LAMB (*downstage*). Spitting on god's mask?

CLARE. They had a winter coat they on't perish.

ADMIRAL. And the poem 'To Mary'. You can't put a book that contains such lines into the hands of a young lady. *I* don't think they're suitable even for the privacy of the bedroom – and I've been round the world twice – but if you choose to think of Mrs Clare as –

MARY LAMB. The tomatoes were quite blue. You find dust everywhere.

REFEREE. Right, lads.

*Round Eight starts.*

MRS EMMERSON. There's a mistake. Clare is married to Patty.

ADMIRAL. Then the poem *must* come out.

## The Fight

FIRST BACKER. Blood on his gob! Pump the fella's tummy up in his mouth.

SECOND BACKER. Let the fella taste what he had for dinner.

FOURTH BACKER. O dear.

SECOND BACKER. Stand him straight before you hit him.

PORTER *knocks* JACKSON *down.* JACKSON *forces himself to stand.*

FIRST BACKER. And again.

> JACKSON *is half unconscious.* PORTER *knocks him down. He sways slowly to his feet, like a half-drowned man forcing himself to make useless gestures. He's unable to give up.*

ADMIRAL (*politely*). Well done the black man! Had them on our ships. Go to pieces in a storm – all whites of eyes and flashing teeth – but put a cutlass in their hands and bellow at them – what soldiers! Counter attack the devil! Used them against Boney!

MRS EMMERSON (*waving a handkerchief at* PORTER). Bravo the navy!

SECOND BACKER. Thrash the bleeder!

FIRST BACKER. Insolent celtic puppy. Take his feet off the ground. Make him soar. No better sight than watching them knocked through the air.

> JACKSON *drifts to his feet.*

THIRD BACKER. Up! Up! Up!

FOURTH BACKER (*to* CLARE. *Slyly amused. Nods at* THIRD BACKER). My young friend cuts his losses every round the Paddy lasts.

MARY LAMB (*takes a loaf from the ornamental bag*). This loaf smells of onions. (*Sniffs it.*) Can it be onions? It goes back.

> PORTER *knocks* JACKSON *out.*

FIRST BACKER. O class.

SECOND BACKER. What a fight! What a man! An ox!

MARY LAMB. Our shopping, Charles. (*She clutches the ornamental bag threateningly.*) Charles, I feel quite ill.

MRS EMMERSON. Should he see a doctor?

ADMIRAL. He'll only be out a few seconds. Even after that.

LAMB (*to* CLARE). She was shopping three times yesterday. A houseful of food. Rotting on the floor. Is she afraid of starving? Is it some punishment? I can't eat it. The rats are so fat they stroll over it. The cost!

MRS EMMERSON (*to* ADMIRAL). I must get tickets for Covent Garden tonight. Mr Corri has set one of Clare's poems to music.

## The Fight

FIRST BACKER (*empties a bottle over* PORTER). Hail!

PORTER. I feel so good an cool lord-suh. I could eat myself. (*Licks wine from his arms.*) Yuh I doo taste sweet.

FIRST BACKER (*slaps* PORTER'S *shoulder*). You're a genius Porter. (*To* SECOND BACKER.) Collect my winnin's from my young shopkeeper friend.

SECOND BACKER *goes to* THIRD *and* FOURTH BACKERS.

PORTER. Exercise! I ain't had my proper exercise chasin' that boy round the grass. (*Laughs.*) Who want a little box? Yes suh!

THIRD BACKER. I'll give you a promissory note.

SECOND BACKER. Last fella welched on the marquis broke both arms goin' home.

THIRD BACKER *pays* SECOND BACKER. JACKSON *gets to his feet.*

THIRD BACKER (*to* JACKSON). A hundred guineas on you! Borrowed money.

FIRST BACKER. We'll take Porter out to dinner – (*Takes* money from SECOND BACKER.) – on this.

REFEREE, PORTER *and* FIRST *and* SECOND BACKERS *go out.*

CLARE (*to* FOURTH BACKER). Yoo lost too?

FOURTH BACKER (*slyly*). Put your money where it works. (*Gestures towards* THIRD BACKER.) Young spark knows it all. Can't learn – 'cept the hard way. (*Smiles.*) I backed the black man.

LAMB (*to* MARY). One shop. Mrs Emmerson. Sir. Clare.

ADMIRAL. Clare. Those lines: out!

MARY LAMB *bows and goes out with* CHARLES.

THIRD BACKER (*to* FOURTH BACKER). Sammy, I paid for his
straw and oats and water. See me through Sammy. Fifty
quid?

FOURTH BACKER. More broke than you are old man. I went in
for his stablin' too remember. You'll earn a few quid if you ain'
particular.

THIRD BACKER *goes out.* FOURTH BACKER *helps* JACKSON
*to dress.*

JACKSON. Me gut. Jazuschriss he must chew granite for breakfast.

CLARE. Wow! Seen knockin' at fairs but I on't see a man git to his
feet after *that*! On't knew a man could stand so much!

JACKSON. Can yous spare a bob sir? If yous enjoyed your fight
yous ought t'pay.

CLARE. On't in the money.

JACKSON. A new coat on your back.

CLARE. That were give us.

JACKSON. Were that give us now? Wish t'god someone'd give me
summat!

MRS EMMERSON. John, the Admiral's tea! And Covent Garden
tonight. You shall learn Mr Corri's tune and whistle it to Patty.

MRS EMMERSON *and the* ADMIRAL *go out.*

CLARE. Did he hurt yoo, boy?

JACKSON. What bloody stupid English question is that? D'you
think I have no feelin's?

CLARE. You kep comin' back.

JACKSON. Then aren't I the bigger fool? Stayed down a sight
bloody sooner if Sammy the hawk hadn't had his eye on me.

FOURTH BACKER (*smiles*). You cost me a packet Paddy but I
don't hold a grudge.

JACKSON *is dressed. He goes out with* FOURTH BACKER.
CLARE *follows* MRS EMMERSON *and the* ADMIRAL.

## SCENE SIX

CLARE's *garden at Northborough.*
*Morning. Pleasant late summer.*
*Table, bench, small fence. House off left.* CLARE *sits at the table. A scrap of paper in front of him. He doesn't write.*

PATTY (*off*). Mr Fab want help. Grubbin' up his ol' orchard an' burn it.

> PATTY *comes on and goes straight to the bench.*

Why on't you goo down an' git took on? Worth a few bob. Time you git down someone else'll hev it.

> PATTY *picks up the basin from the bench and goes into the house.*

(*Off.*) Tired a you sit under my feet all day. Scribble bits a paper. No one on't bother read all that. Thought you was supposed a be clever boy. I'm daft but I know *that*.

> PATTY *comes out of the house. She carries the basin with water, potatoes and a knife in it.*

Scrap *them* boy. Sit there you make yourself useful. On't take much a your time. On't enough for that. On't scrap em thick. Make a proper job.

> CLARE *moves his paper to one side. He starts to peel the potatoes.* PATTY *goes into the house.*

(*Off.*) Shall *I* goo down Fab's an' ask? He were a mate a mine fore I wed. Spot a hard work doo you good boy. Sweat the scribble out a you.

> CLARE *pulls the piece of paper towards him and suddenly writes very quickly.* PATTY *comes out of the house and watches in silence.* CLARE *finishes writing before he answers.*

CLARE. Smell a burnin'd lay on my stomach. You know I on't kip nothin down.

PATTY. Nothin t'kip down! (*Looks at paper. Reads slowly.*) That say Mary? (*Knowingly.*) I'll catch her out one day. (*Slight pause.*) On't a letter? (*No answer.*) Who is she boy?

CLARE. Gall.

PATTY. Had 'nough sense not t'wed yoo. On't that bake house gall at Maxey? (*No answer.*) One a your London madams.

CLARE. She on't round no more.

PATTY. On't see the point a writin t'someone when they on't round no more even if that is poetry.

BABY *starts to cry in the house.*

She goo in your new book? Allus in your books. What do next-door think? Bin your doormat too long. (*Calls to* BABY.) Chuck chuck darlint. Your ol' mum on't far.

CLARE. There on't a new book.

PATTY. Bin scribblin day-in-day-out for years. House full a it! On't that nough for a new book yit?

CLARE. No new book. Last book on't sold.

PATTY. What?

CLARE *starts to peel the potatoes.*

Told me they like how you write up London.

CLARE. No more books.

PATTY. Well – thank chriss for that! So thass all over then? Now we know where you stand. On't scrap them too thick.

PATTY *goes into the house.* CLARE *goes on peeling potatoes and dipping them in the water.*

(*Off,* she tries to control her happiness.) Can't say I on't said. No surprise t'me. Well now you know who stick by you. Put all that ol' scribble in a big box. I'll scrounge one off the shop. No call t'throw 'em out. Never know. Someday someone might want a buy one. (*To* BABY.) There now shall mummy make him comfy? (*To* CLARE.) God hang the man that invented ink. Wicked shame. Let 'em lead you a proper dance boy. Times I told you what it'd be. You?: no, wouldn't hev it. Well, thass done with. Best thing all round. Now our luck's beginnin' t'change.

PATTY *comes out of the house. She carries the* BABY.

On't say *I* on't grateful. (*Picks up the piece of paper.*) Put her with the rest?

CLARE (*after a slight pause*) . . . Leave it . . .

PATTY (*frightened*). Thass over boy.

CLARE. Ont goo back labourin'. On't know what I'm at out in the fields. (*Picks up his pen.*) Goo sit back the hedge an' write on me hat. Who'd give us work?

PATTY. Fab for a start.

CLARE. How long that last? Week?

PATTY. Hev t'kip askin'. Got work last harvest. Lads'll jike you first off. They'll soon git tired. On't never give yourself airs.

CLARE. Can't live like that. Can't help what I am. God know I wish I couldn't write me name! But my mind git full a songs an' I on't feel a man if I on't write 'em down. O god I on't even know if thass truth anymore. (*Throws pen down.*) No grip left in me hand! Pain in me head! Gut burn! Thass terrible gall.

PATTY. On't try git round me. My sympathy run out years agoo. On't fed right. Thass all the matter with you. Bring regular wages in the house an' I'll soon hev you fed up. Forgit Mary an' think a me. On't rowin. One kid on my hands an' another on the way. Tired a all this self. You think a someone else. Feed *us*. Thass your job boy. On't goo out workin' while I'm carryin'. An' they on't let you on the parish while you got your health.

CLARE. Health gall? My limbs're on fire?

PATTY. On't talk so daft! Talk straight so a body can hev a proper conversation. If you're on fire you goo up in smoke. On'y smoke I seen out a you's tobacco – when you scrounge it. (*To* CHILD.) There there, ol' mum on't row *you*. (*To* CLARE.) Limbs! Normal people hev arms an' legs. Chriss sake talk like a man. On't comfortable with you in the house. Talk like some little ol' gall so well brought up she can't git her gloves off without the footman. Aches an' pains? I'll know what smartin' is when I hev your kid.

CLARE (*hands her the basin*). Done.

PATTY (*takes the basin. She now holds the basin and the child*). Sick t'death a the whole bloody thing! Like a new pair a shoes like other women doo. A shirt. Or a bit a ribboned. I'm still a

young woman. Sit down to a decent meal. Just once. Tired a
hoardin' every little scrap t'make it look like a proper meal.
Sick an' tired. I'll tell you why you're ill: you're hangin'
about atwix an atween. No mystery there. You on't know what
you're supposed t'be at. No wonder you're sick. All that scribble
scribble drive anyone sick. An' for what? For Chriss sake what?
They on't even read it! Look at this child John Clare. Thass
sick an' pukin since it come in the world – cause thass famished
like its mother. An its father. An' we're famished for what?
Scribble scribble scribble on bits a paper for rats t'eat! Scribble
scribble scribble scribble.

> CLARE *turns away.* PATTY *puts the basin down.*

On't turn your back on me! Tell you straight boy: had enough.
I goo down Fab's an' git you took on. (*She picks up the basin.*)
You borrow a saw next door an' goo down six t'morra sharp
an' show willin'. Or you on't sleep an' eat by my side. I'll
shame you.

> PATTY *takes the basin into the house.* CLARE *sits and stares in
> front of him. Pause.* MRS EMMERSON *comes through the gate.
> She carries a canvas bag.*

CLARE. Mrs Emmerson . . .
MRS EMMERSON. Good day, John.
CLARE. What're you dooin' here?

> CLARE *gets up and goes to her. He moves like an old man.*

MRS EMMERSON. I didn't warn you. You'd have got into one of
your fusses.

> CLARE *impulsively puts his arms round her and starts to cry.*

CLARE. O mam . . . mam . . . Five years. No one t'talk to. I'm so
alone. (*Takes his arms from her.*) Sorry. Mustn't. Sit down.
(*Cleans the bench.*) Sit here.
MRS EMMERSON. You look ill. So tired, John.
CLARE (*puzzled.*) But I warned you. Put everythin' in my letters.
My stomach an' my hands. My mind goo dead.
MRS EMMERSON. But suddenly seeing you.

PATTY (*off*). Hope someone enjoy your scribble. God know I suffered for it.

CLARE. What's the London news? You on't sit down. Had a letter from my publisher –

MRS EMMERSON. I know.

CLARE. He'll hev t'change his mind mam. On't nothin' t'live on bar my books.

PATTY (*off*.) Sleep on your own after this. You hev the pleasure a getting kids you hev the worry a feedin 'em.

CLARE. I'll tell Patty. She'll want t'smarten up fore you see her. Sit down.

> CLARE *hurries into the house.* MRS EMMERSON *looks round. She puts her bag by the table. She sits on the bench. She reads the poem.* CLARE *comes out of the house.*

MRS EMMERSON. It's as I imagined. Full of peace and stillness.

CLARE. Where you put up?

MRS EMMERSON. Lord Milton's.

CLARE. Oh.

MRS EMMERSON. He's coming here now. I came ahead. I wanted to have a little time with you. On our own.

CLARE. What he want?

MRS EMMERSON. Did you know how I looked forward to your London visits? (*Smiles.*) You were –. When my husband died, our talks were – well, almost my reason for living. You still write?

CLARE. Hundreds a verse. Chorus in my head all day. Each one sing a different tune. Struggle t'git one straight at a time.

MRS EMMERSON. You write too much.

CLARE. Patty'd say yes t'that. Scare her. Like hevin a drunk in the house. Moaned when I drank a bit over the edge. Now it's the words – an' they're worse. (*Moves bag.*) She's heavy. Lug that all on your own?

MRS EMMERSON (*smiles at the paper*). More Mary?

CLARE. My other wife.

MRS EMMERSON. Have you turned Mohammedan, John?

CLARE. Not my real wife. No she is real. But not Patty. My other real wife.

MRS EMMERSON. It's a bag of your books. They won't sell. The publisher's let you have them cost price. That will help you. Take them round your neighbours.

CLARE. But the village on't read.

MRS EMMERSON. There'll be easier to sell where you're known.

CLARE. They on't read woman! Barrin' the parson and a few others – an' they got copies!

MRS EMMERSON. John, you must co-operate with your friends when they try to help you. Don't – (*She searches for an idiom.*) – fly off the handle. Surely *visitors* would gladly purchase a copy at the –

CLARE. On't git visitors now! An' the few that doo come expect a copy free for the trouble a findin' me out! That letter from my publisher – he sold all they books – first book give him three editions – he say I owe *him* money! Hundred an' forty pound! Work on the land you git ten bob a week. On't live on that let alone pay him! Now he dump this on me an say cost price! Cost? Cost? That cost me the earth!

MRS EMMERSON. Publishing is a business. Printing, advertising, copies for critics –

CLARE. Hev the world gone mad? No wonder they say I'm a clown!

MRS EMMERSON. Preparing the text. You don't even punctuate. Your penchant for native words. The foreign languages your readers know are Latin and Greek – not East Anglian! Your – scribble has to be decoded and made accessible to polite society. That has to be paid for.

CLARE. Lord Radstock.

MRS EMMERSON. He's written to your publishers.

CLARE. Lord Milton.

MRS EMMERSON. I'd help, but my husband left so little. He was an invalid and I was never a good manager. A widow of my social standing can't risk any suggestion of want ... Society is so intolerant.

CLARE. Patty you had long enough!

PATTY *comes out of the house immediately. She has straightened her clothes and washed. She stands stiffly by the door.*

MRS EMMERSON. I shall call you Patty straight away.

PATTY (*bobs awkwardly*). Yes'm.

CLARE. Show her Fred.

PATTY (*defensively*). Sleepin'.

MRS EMMERSON. Later. I'm at Milton House for a few days.

PATTY. Yes'm.

MRS EMMERSON. It's a difficult joy being married to a great writer. You're lucky to be the woman in his house.

PATTY. (*to* CLARE). She askin' for a cup a tea?

CLARE (*opens the book and hides his face in it*). All these pages. On'y the author's read 'em. Opened 'em.

MRS EMMERSON. Don't cry on them, John. No one will buy if they're soiled. Show me your new work.

CLARE. Us'll hev t'git a proper job. Somethin' drastic t'bring in proper money. Set up boxin'. They git paid for bein' knocked about. I git knock about. Why on't I paid for it? I know the back a your faces: think I on't up to it. I'd surprise you.

CLARE *goes into the house.* PATTY *tries to follow.*

MRS EMMERSON. Patty our women's talk.

PATTY *stops.*

Well?

PATTY. Pardon'm?

MRS EMMERSON. How is he?

PATTY. On't know'm.

MRS EMMERSON. He still thinks he's a boxer.

PATTY. Sometime'm.

MRS EMMERSON. You don't let him drink?

PATTY (*laughs with nerves so that she snorts*). What on? No one treat him now.

MRS EMMERSON. Lord Milton's coming.

PATTY. Now?

MRS EMMERSON. Don't be alarmed. They'll do what's best. If he has to go into care they'll take him today.

PATTY. That soon'm?

MRS EMMERSON. Surely? If he needs help he must have it before his mind's irretrievably lost. Untoward delays can be fatal.

PATTY. So soon.

MRS EMMERSON. Let us pray in a year this is all over. John will be home again. Well enough to work and support his family.

PATTY. On't know'm.

MRS EMMERSON. Even now all might yet go well. If only you surround him with assurance and support. Surely he can find peace in this garden? (*She stares at the view.*)

PATTY. Yes'm. (*Slight pause.*) Baby cry. Gentry stay all hours. On't seem t'realise you hev t'git up of a mornin' ... beggin' your pardon'm. That an' the worry.

MRS EMMERSON (*turns to* PATTY. *Uncertain.*) What, dear?

PATTY. The doctor ought a see his pains by right. God knows I on't want him t'goo. Shut up here on my own. He say a visit t'London'd help. But he hev t'come back an' that make it worse. Seen it afore.

MRS EMMERSON. You have this garden. This beautiful view.

PATTY. I look at that an' think a the rent. On't goo an' see him. Hope none a you expect that.

MRS EMMERSON. Patty.

PATTY. Even if had the fare. On't manage. On't my world. Gentry come here scare me. Hev n'more on it. Never bin off more'n a few miles. How I goo trapsin' round a city askin' strangers the way t'the *madhouse*? On't doo more'n I can.

MRS EMMERSON. You married him.

PATTY. On't-ought-a-had by rights. How'd I know what it'd turn out t'be? He on't harm a fly. But what use is that to us?

LORD MILTON *and* PARSON *come in.* LORD MILTON *carries two canvas bags and the* PARSON *one. They put them beside* MRS EMMERSON's *bag.*

MILTON. How've you got on Ellen?

MRS EMMERSON. We had our talk.

MILTON. Doctor's down the lane. I brought my keeper in case of trouble. Didn't want to all descend at once.

PARSON. Clare's wife.

MILTON. Afternoon Mrs. Clare. (PATTY *stands stock still.*) Shan't intrude. I'll keep my visit short.

MRS EMMERSON. It's good of you to find the time. We know this touches you as much as us.

CLARE *comes out of the house.*

PARSON. Good afternoon. Clare. Lord Milton's here to see you. Be on your best behaviour. A credit to the village.

CLARE. On'y got the one behaviour so he'll hev t'make doo. Others hev. On't lookin' for a scrap with the church. (*Makes a boxing gesture.*) You bin in some scraps. Gen'man climb in the ring from time t'time t'defend his title. (*Laughs*). Her dead brother Darkie know. Hev his lordship come for a book? Can hev one cheap. Lower than London rates. Take two or more an' you git a discount. Or if he's hard up like us – thass bad times – tell him I'll let him hev a soil one cheap. Letters smudge but thass still fit t'read. (*Turns to get a book and sees the four bags.*) Four! My word the power of the press! The gospel's spread. The word bore fruit.

*Turns back to the others. He becomes quiet and laconic.*

Will his lordship take tea? Patty make a good cup a cottage tea. Burnt bread in hot water an pepper t'taste. That on't take t'sugar. (*Slight pause.*) Words, my lord. You hev a poet in your parish parson. You had a poet in your field my lord. Wrote first poem when I were a boy pickin' up stones in your field. Took a stone in me hand an' a poem come in me head.

MRS EMMERSON. Show us your lovely new poem.

CLARE. 'My Mary'?

PARSON. Who *is* she?

CLARE. My wife. My real wife. Not Patty but my other wife. (*To* PATTY.) On't you frit my darlint. Had nowt t'doo with her for years. Look her out all place but she on't be found. Gone. I on't her choosin'. Or likely I doo us both wrong an' she's in the ground. On't Patty's fault she on't the gal I want. Bin a good wife. Good mother. Stood by me. But how'd I live with her? No, I remember *her*: the other one. An' all I want's t'lay my head on her breast. Peace then. Laugh agin. Talk like a sensible man. I'm so alone.

MILTON *nods to the* PARSON. *The* PARSON *goes towards the gate.*

Parson aren't you old! Lie in your churchyard soon stead a lyin' in your church. An ol' man's hair's the colour a bone. Seen 'em stack outside the slaughter house. Goo t'be turned t'glue. Seen a mouse once. Made its home in the heap a' bones an' shoulder blades stood outside the door. There'd bin some bellowin' that day! Slaughter a whole herd. Ox. O he were proud on his little house. Pop in an' out. Took seed in the hole.

*The* PARSON *goes.*

(*Gestures at* PARSON). He reeks. Glue.
MILTON. Read us a poem.
CLARE. I hev – but you on't know how t'listen. On't write for you. On't be a poet then. No more'n his carpenter's a carpenter. He touch a piece a wood an' it turn t'coffin. His corn's grass. His men are animals – goo round an' round his house on a rope, on a path shape like a sover-in. – I waited an' no one come, or give tuppence without a grudge. An' what I wrote was good. Yes. Worth readin'. Shall I step in line now? No. I on't labour in your fields n'more. Labour in my fields. You cut your fields up small so you could eat 'em better. I've eat my portion of the universe an' I shall die of it. It was bitter fruit. But I had more out the stones in your field than you had out the harvest.

*The* PARSON *and* DR SKRIMSHIRE *come in.*

PARSON. Clare, this is Dr Skrimshire. Your friends are worried about your pains and stories –
CLARE. Patty!
PATTY. Had me up parson's. Had t'tell what you say. Bein' a boxer an' Lord Byron.
CLARE. Patty thass just men I saw in London! (*Immediately turns to* DOCTOR.) Doctor I doo hev pains in my head! It git covered in boils. Sometimes I start t'goo blind. When I write. Why is that? My head were that hot this mornin'.

MILTON. Painful to see you in this distress. Unlike yourself. Let the doctor help you. I shall meet all expense. Mr Twice, as representative of the parish.

PARSON (*nods*). My lord.

MILTON. Mrs Emmerson, you're a close friend.

MRS EMMERSON. If the doctor can help.

DOCTOR (*looking at* CLARE). Mr Clare should spend a few months with me. At the end of that time I shall begin to know him. Then I can start disentangling the truth from the poetry. (*Smiles seriously.*) If things went well you'd soon be back. Rest and quiet are sometimes difficult to get at home.

KEEPER *comes to the gate.*

CLARE. Where's your hospital?

DOCTOR. My lord when a mind's poised on the brink of grotesque oblivion it must not be offended with lies. (*To* CLARE.) I run a house for the mentally ill. Outside London. I don't lock my patients up or punish them. That's already been tried before they come to me. Your wife needs a rest too. Is she carrying?

MRS EMMERSON. Patty, we'll go into the house.

PATTY. On't budge.

CLARE. Out a my garden! I managed till now –

MRS EMMERSON. John, you haven't managed!

CLARE. Git out!

MILTON *grabs at* CLARE *and finds himself pinioning him with his arms. There is a shocked silence.* MILTON *stops in surprise and lets* CLARE *go.*

MILTON. O. (*To* KEEPER *in sudden anger.*) You!

KEEPER *takes* CLARE. *He winds a short rope round his arms and chest.*

CLARE. You can't drag me out my garden! Let us goo!

KEEPER *takes him to the gate.*

My kid. My papers, Mrs Emmerson! Patty, fetch next-door! (*Calls.*) I'll start work. Call Fab. Patty.

KEEPER. Settle down in the cart.

CLARE (*as he's led off*). Mrs Kemp dear! Git my brothers out the field!

*The* KEEPER *takes* CLARE *away.* PATTY *watches in silence.* MRS EMMERSON *cries.*

MILTON. He was so slight. Skin and bone. Like a quail.

PARSON (*looks at his watch*). I'm old. My mind was settled on death long ago. But god sends me home to sleep in my own house.

MILTON. I'll drop you. (*To* PATTY.) Goodbye. I'll have the empty bags collected.

MILTON *goes out.*

PARSON (*to* PATTY). Come when you need anything. My sister will look in. The world is in shadow because the father stoops so low to nurse his children. (*Shrugs.*) No, no one understands ... Tragedy is like justice, blind and over pity. Clare didn't ask for help. He scorned us ... In a way his sufferings condemn him. They protect him with the arrogance of a certain sort of pain.

PARSON *goes out.*

MRS EMMERSON. Shall I call the neighbours?

PATTY. T'on't necessary. They'll look in. Feed baby or that'll fret. (*Picks up the poem.*) Will you take it? I could let you hev a handful. He'd expect me t'ask.

MRS EMMERSON. No ... perhaps later.

PATTY. Was he a proper writer?

MRS EMMERSON. One's partiality blinds one. At first – but perhaps they became only ramblings, droolings ... (*Cries.*) O this terrible day! He was so brave. He did so much – (*Hanky.*) but he couldn't even get a living like any rough you see hanging about the lanes. Why? (*She tears her hanky in anger.*) I'm sorry.

*She takes coins from her purse and gives them to* PATTY. PATTY *goes into the house.*

MRS EMMERSON (*dabbing eyes*). Torn hanky.

MRS EMMERSON *puts the hanky away and goes out.* PATTY *comes out of the house. She feeds the baby at her breast.*

PATTY. Dig that. Few rows. Tatties an greens. Mind you grow up quick an' be a help. Us'll cope. Mary? Mary who? What Mary? On't come back n'more. Pair on em. Mary on't drive the sense out your head boy.

*She strokes the* BABY's *head.*

Safe now. An' your playmate. (*Taps stomach.*) His books learn you how t'starve. On't need books t'learn that. Mary.

## SCENE SEVEN

*Open space.*
*Night.*
*The* BOXER *sits on a boundary post, hunched forward in the pose of The Thinker.* CLARE *comes in. He is exhausted and in rags.*

CLARE (*calls routinely*). Mary? (*Sighs.*) Walked so far . . . (*Sees* BOXER.) The Paddy! Still fightin' boy – or just dead?

MARY *comes on. She is a tramp. Grotesque, filthy, ugly.*

Mary.
MARY. What?
CLARE. Mary. At last.
MARY. On't make a game a me boy!
CLARE. It's John.
MARY. Who?
CLARE. John Clare.
MARY. I on't . . . Yes! – boy got me sacked out the big house! You changed boy. Terrible old.
CLARE. They locked me up.
MARY. Prison?
CLARE. Like a prison. Four years. Then I run for it. Come lookin' for you.
MARY. Why?

CLARE. I thought a you all the time. On't you think a me?

MARY. Can't say I hev.

CLARE. We was wed.

MARY. On't talk so far back! How'd you look after me? (*Laughs.*) He's hard done by? Lives like a Lord! *I* live like an animal with its hide pull off.

CLARE (*puts his hand on his crutch*). I'm still strong.

MARY (*laughs*). Look at him! Want summat a sight more appetizin' fore I put myself out this time a night. Bin on the road how many days an' what you had t' eat?

CLARE. Some grass. Taste a bread.

MARY. Grass! I look the sort a woman goo with a chap that eat grass? Hell-a-bit! I still git little better class'n escape convict.

CLARE. Marry me.

MARY. Take your hand off yourself. Cut you open doo you bother me.

CLARE. I give it all away for you. Patty, kids, home, my whole life. All away. I had you once. Lived all my life off that. Always hev you in my head. Watchin', talkin', smilin'. All the time. Good an' bad. Never git tired. Never lose hope. Everything goo t'gither in you. An' all those years my life was waste. You on't there. On'y in my head. That drove me mad. I'd a stood the rest with you. Now you're here an' you say . . . No, I'm tougher'n you think! Show how I fight. (*Turns to* BOXER.) Hey up, Paddy!

*Stands in a boxing pose in front of the* BOXER, *dances on his toes.*

Sat there long enough an' on't fall down – stand up two minutes till I knock you down!

*Punches the* BOXER's *arm.*

Lady want a scrap!

*The* BOXER *looks up. It is* DARKIE. *He has a burn mark on his neck.*

Darkie . . . They hang you boy!

DARKIE. On't see too well. Tell the truth the boxin' give me a squint an' I goo blind. Punch punch or summat – knock all the sight out my head. Sorry if you're an acquaintance. The discourtesy on't intended.

CLARE. Darkie it's John Clare.

DARKIE. John? What you punch my arm for?

CLARE. I'm sorry Darkie I on't –

DARKIE (*groping for him*). On't make a sport a me!

*Tries to hit* CLARE *but can't find him.*

Come on!

CLARE. No Darkie. On't know you're blind.

DARKIE. You jabber. I'll git you.

CLARE (*trying to help him*). No Darkie! Sit down ol' chap. Let me . . .

*DARKIE catches him on the side of the head.* CLARE *half falls.*

DARKIE. That hit summat!

CLARE (*doubles over*). Don't Darkie! Don't!

*DARKIE throws a violent punch and misses. He throws another and catches* CLARE'*s head.* CLARE *passes out.*

DARKIE. An' that! 'Nough boy? (*He gropes round for* CLARE.) Hev he pass out?

MARY (*looking at* CLARE). Knock out by a blind boy? You're all trouble an' no joy! (*To* DARKIE.) I goo off with anyone I'll goo off with you. You're a better piece of flesh than him.

DARKIE (*sitting on the stone marker*). On't git far with me. They torment you for a laugh when you're blind. Need all my strength t'crack their heads. On't eat. No grub for years. Sit here an' try t'forgit. But the cravin goo on.

MARY. I got bread.

DARKIE (*holds out his hands*). Where? Where?

*MARY takes out bread and gives it to him.*

Hev you got a whole loaf! (*Chews.*) Jaw stiff.

MARY. You dribble like an ol' man.

DARKIE (*chewing*). On't kip in. (*Calmly.*) Chew an' chew but on't

know how t'swallow. My gullet's set. (*In tears.*) I'm hungry an'
I can't swallow.

MARY (*feeds him.*) Here boy. Try.

DARKIE. Summat in my neck. Summat goo crosst or thass a
twist. Can't eat.

MARY (*holding bread in his mouth*). Be a good chap.

DARKIE. My mouth taste a bread –

MARY. Try –

DARKIE – but I can't eat. It hurt. It hurt.

> DARKIE *spits out the bread. It sprays on the floor.*

MARY. Risk my life for that!

DARKIE (*holds his neck*). My neck! Hurt!

MARY. Hush boy! Listen! (*Silence.*) Someone there. Quick. Out
the road. Hide till thass safe.

> MARY *takes* DARKIE *off upstage.* THREE IRISHMEN *come in:*
> FIRST *is older than* SECOND *and* THIRD. *They're muffled in
> dark clothes. They carry bundles, parcels and sticks.*

FIRST IRISHMAN. This hollow lads. Sleep here. It's dry. Get
the water on the fire. We'll go on to Bourne t'morra. There's
work there.

> FIRST IRISHMAN *starts to light a fire.* THIRD IRISHMAN
> *fills the kettle.*

THIRD IRISHMAN. I'll never git rich: I work too bloody hard.

SECOND IRISHMAN. Give us your mug Tommy. And give us the
kettle here. His tea taste like piss out the udder of a dead cow.

FIRST IRISHMAN. If they bring any more machines on the land
they won't need us. When the harvest's over we'll try the
railroads. Buildin' railroads every bloody where.

THIRD IRISHMAN. You'd think they wanted t' travel away from
theirselves. Iron trains, iron houses, iron cannons. They sleep
in iron beds.

SECOND IRISHMAN. What do they think about when they poke
their little women: nails?

THIRD IRISHMAN. I'm not goin' on no railroad. Work like a
bloody steam-engine yourself.

CLARE *stands up.*

SECOND IRISHMAN. Jazuschriss the lord is risen.

CLARE. Cold night.

SECOND IRISHMAN. Where you goin' laddie? Haven't seen your face round here.

FIRST IRISHMAN. Out of prison?

CLARE. T'wont prison.

THIRD IRISHMAN. He's loony in the head.

FIRST IRISHMAN. On your own, is it?

CLARE. Mate's back there. And a woman.

THIRD IRISHMAN. Jazuschriss have you a woman back there? (CLARE *nods.*) Jazus-be-buggered is chriss wastin' women on you when there's a young fella here with his finger pokin up t'catch the chairman's eye? Is she all roight?

CLARE. Ay.

THIRD IRISHMAN. I mean, is she clean?

SECOND IRISHMAN. Jazus he'd hire himself out as a pitchfork t'git stuck in the muck.

THIRD IRISHMAN. How old would she be?

CLARE. My age.

THIRD IRISHMAN. It's a dark night. I'll make you a proposition now. Let me lay down with your little lady an' I'll give you my bread an' cheese. Is it on? Best cheese, my man.

CLARE. Hang on what she say.

THIRD IRISHMAN. If the lady says yes to you she'll say grace when she sees me.

CLARE *takes the bread and cheese. He eats like a starving man.*

FIRST IRISHMAN. Hang on Arny.

*Turns to* CLARE *and holds his arm to stop him eating.*

If your lady's any good it's me an' Michael after. Is that agreed sonny?

THIRD IRISHMAN (*after a slight pause*). Great-roarin-dust haven't we all t'share alike? If that's not in the Bible god slipped up.

FIRST IRISHMAN. And there'll be a mouthful for the lady after.

CLARE *starts eating again.* THIRD IRISHMAN *goes off.* CLARE
*stands and eats. The other* IRISHMEN *watch him.*

SECOND IRISHMAN. Slowly. You won't see Arny a while yit.
(*Slight pause.*) Come up to the fire. (CLARE *steps closer.*) Would
she be blond?
CLARE. Black.
FIRST IRISHMAN. Huha.
SECOND IRISHMAN. Long hair or short?
CLARE. Long.
FIRST IRISHMAN. Huha. An well set up?
CLARE. Huha.
SECOND IRISHMAN. But small inside?
CLARE. Huha.
SECOND IRISHMAN. As Christ's my god I like it small. Where
you make you own room.

*The* KEEPER *comes in. He is the former* ASSISTANT KEEPER.
*He is dressed in dark clothes and carries a gun.*

FIRST IRISHMAN. We're resting quietly mister.
KEEPER. Not on Lord Milton's land.
SECOND IRISHMAN. Jazuschriss a man can't put a road in his
pocket! I tell a lie. They put Ireland.

THIRD IRISHMAN *comes back.* KEEPER *steps into shadows.*

THIRD IRISHMAN. You little lyin' English punk! What bloody
woman?
CLARE (*points off stage*). There. (*Wipes his mouth.*)
THIRD IRISHMAN. You gobbled my bloody supper down smart.
Lyin' git. There's no bloody snatch in that wood. I'd find a
snatch if that's twice as dark as black. Lyin' English git! Don't
play games with me, fella-me-lad. I'll break your bloody neck,
you lying' punk. What's up?
FIRST IRISHMAN. Pol-iss.

KEEPER *empties the kettle over the fire.*

Are we supposed t'walk all night?

KEEPER. Village two mile down the road. On't pay for lodgin's – thass your trouble.

SECOND IRISHMAN. Come to earn not spend. If you had a starvin' family back home you'd understand.

FIRST IRISHMAN. They won't put us up in the village. We take their fellas' jobs. That's how your boss keeps his wages down.

KEEPER. You wake my birds up. His lordship hev a shoot an his London guests on't git a good bag – I'm out. T'on't the easiest job. I got a wife an' nippers too.

*The* IRISHMEN *collect their things.*

THIRD IRISHMAN (*pushing* CLARE *out of his way*). Another twisted thievin' English git.

SECOND IRISHMAN. One night your lord's barn'll go up in flames.

THIRD IRISHMAN. An' his ricks.

FIRST IRISHMAN (*gives* THIRD IRISHMAN *a bundle*). Arny.

SECOND IRISHMAN. An' no one'll put 'em out.

THIRD IRISHMAN *picks up the last bundle. The* THREE IRISHMEN *go out.*

CLARE (*going upstage*). Mary! Mary!

KEEPER. No woman there. I'd hev heard.

CLARE. I dreamt I saw bread spat on the ground, and her say: Waste, I risk my life! (*Shakes his head.*) No. Bread on't waste. Thass on'y seed so you threw it on the ground. Birds hev it. Or that soak away. Bread goo from mouth t'mouth an' what it taste of: other mouths. Talkin' an' laughin'. Thinkin' people. I wandered round an' round. Where to? Here. An' a blind man git here before me. The blind goo in a straight line. We should hev come t'gither. She git the bread. He crack the heads when they come after us. An' I – I'ld hev teach him how to eat. I am a poet an' I teach men how to eat. Then she on't goo in rags. He on't blind. An' I – on't goo mad in a madhouse. No. No one there. Never was. On'y the songs I make up on them ... Walk four days. What, ninety mile? Head git mix up. Patty on't welcome me neither.

KEEPER. Village down –

CLARE. I know where the village is. I'll goo home an' wait quiet,

till they come. Nothin' here now. Nice t'set eyes on my boys.
Tell em t'help their mother. P'raps my sons on't hev me in the
house when they grow up.

KEEPER. Down there. (*Treads on the last of the fire.*) Keep on the
path an' git off the land. Night.

*They go.*

## SCENE EIGHT

*Home.*
*Afternoon.*
*Simple, comfortable room. Chintz armchairs. Big windows. A glass
door set in them. Sunny and pleasant.*

MARY LAMB *sits at a table opposite* NAPOLEON. *They play chess.*
MARY LAMB *makes a move. Silence.* NAPOLEON *makes a move.*

NAPOLEON. That's the move I made at Austerlitz.
Wellington won because he'd learned to cheat on the playing
fields of Eton.

*They stare at the game in silence. They don't move. The door
opens.* DOCTOR SKRIMSHIRE *shows* LORD MILTON *in.*
LORD MILTON *wears brick-red tweeds and carries a cane.*

DOCTOR (*nervously*). If your lordship waits in here.

MILTON. Pleasant room.

DOCTOR. The south facing drawing room. If I'd known your
lordship was –

MILTON. Spur of the moment.

DOCTOR. Was there any special reason for ...? (*His voice trails
away in anxiety.*)

MILTON. I was asked to.

DOCTOR *starts to go.* MILTON *stops him.*

Will he recognise me?

DOCTOR. He may. Er, sometimes they're full of complaints, and
another time everything's fine – so you mustn't take ... (*He
stops awkwardly.*) Won't you sit down?

DOCTOR SKRIMSHIRE *goes.* MILTON *walks towards the chess.*

MILTON. A demanding game.

> *They ignore him.* MARY LAMB *makes a move.* MILTON *wanders to the windows. He looks out.*

Beautiful grounds. Elms. Shadows on the lawn. Reminds me of home. Will *I* recognise *him?*

MARY LAMB. Don't use the soap. It smells.

MILTON. O I'm only a visitor, not . . . D'you know Mr Clare?

MARY LAMB. He doesn't get visitors. And they don't let him out. Took his key away. Years ago. A girl in the church porch. The mother complained.

> *The door opens. A man in a straight-jacket is pushed into the room. He is old, grey, dressed in grey, and completely unrecognisable. He makes rhythmic sounds. A* KEEPER *follows him. The man writhes from side to side but doesn't resist being propelled. His neck is stretched stiff.*

MAN IN STRAIT-JACKET. Mmm! Mmm! Mmm! Mmm! Mmm! Hup! Mmm! Mmm! Mmm! Mmm!

> *The* KEEPER *propels him over the room and out the other side. A moment later* DOCTOR SKRIMSHIRE *appears in the open doorway.*

DOCTOR. So sorry my lord. Fixing the decorations for the autumn ball. He got into a tizzy.

> DOCTOR SKRIMSHIRE *turns round and pushes* CLARE *into the room. He's in a bathchair. A shrivelled puppet. His head nods like a doll's. His face is white.*

Takes him time to wake up. (*To* CLARE.) Visitor John.

MILTON. Leave us alone.

DOCTOR. Of course. (*Hesitates.*) If your lordship would care to take tea in our rooms? A meat tea. I would be most –

MILTON. How kind.

DOCTOR. I'll alert my wife.

> *The* DOCTOR *hurries out.*

MILTON. Sorry. Didn't mean to wake you. D'you need anything? (*Silence.*) It's a nice garden.

*Silence.* NAPOLEON *makes a move.*

Can you remember Mrs Emmerson? She died last week. When they confined her to bed she wrote and asked me to see you. D'you remember us? Seeing you brings it back. The afternoon in your garden. So long ago. Another world. The estate went to church every Sunday. I sat in front in my high pew. The parson read the story of the centurion. The man with authority. I say to this man, Go, and he goeth; and to another come, and he cometh. So be it done unto thee. The Bible. *You* had some books out too. Time to write here? No. It's changed. The village is there. But new houses. Part of the town really. (*Pause.*) What else? I can't sleep. See my wife's grave from the windows. Lie awake. Through the night. The dawn hurts my eyes. I hate my son. A vicious bastard. I was cruel sometimes. Foolish. But did I hate? No. Never a hater. He hates. Flicks his wrist as if he's holding a whip. Don't see much of him – except his back. Busy. In love with his factories. It's changed. D'you know who I am?

CLARE. Ha . . . yer . . .

MARY LAMB (*interpreting*). A new shirt.

MILTON. Yes. Anything else? (*Silence.*) Your wife's downstairs. Wouldn't come up. The journey upset her. Asked me to check first. You ought to see her. She's come a long way. Can I go down here?

> MILTON *opens the door in the windows and goes out. He disappears. The door swings slowly open. It catches the sun. It flashes once into the room. Brilliantly. Silence. An owl calls in the trees.*

NAPOLEON (*calls*). Poet – this is Napoleon. He's fetching your wife. (*Slight pause. To* MARY LAMB.) He's a government spy. He watched my strategy. I fooled him.

CLARE. Wh . . . yer . . . yer . . .

MARY LAMB (*interpreting*). He said What's she like?

NAPOLEON (*looks through window*). Nice little old lady. In black. Bent. Grey hair.

MARY LAMB. Ask him for soap and give it to me. Or I'll tell your wife about the little girl.

*Pause.* MILTON *and* PATTY *come through the open door in the windows.*

MILTON. Talk. (*He stands by the windows.*)

PATTY. On't want t'come. On't know how you'd feel. Bin twenty-three years. He say I had to. Brought you some a your apple jelly. Apple off your crab tree. (*Pause. Tries to jolly him along.*) Hear you're gettin' a new shirt. There! They all send love.

*No reply. She goes to* MILTON.

I'll goo home now if you can give me a lift.

MILTON. He's shy. Talk to him.

PATTY (*goes back to* CLARE). Good garden this year. Best sprouts for a long time. Proper journey gettin' here. On't used t'travel. Not like you allus gallivantin' up t'London. (*Terser.*) Well on't you least gooin' say hello, boy? Let's see some a the ol' self.

CLARE. Ha . . . m . . . m . . . b . . .

MARY LAMB (*interpreting*). How are his boys?

PATTY (*goes to* MILTON). Askin' after his boys. Sent a letter when they died. (*Goes back to* CLARE.) You remember your letter? Said they had good funerals an' names on the grave. Anythin' you want?

CLARE. G . . . g . . . g . . .

MARY LAMB. Go home.

PATTY. Here's home now. 'S all changed. New next-door. Nice here. Waited on. Regular food. Kep' clean an dry. I see they on't put you in the poor wing.

CLARE. T . . . t . . . b . . . w . . .

MARY LAMB. Tell the boys to write.

PATTY (*tries to jolly him*). Come by train. There! You on't bin on a train with all your gadding' about. Line goo by the village. Goo out Sunday evenin's an' see the trains. The sparks doo goo! There!

CLARE. B . . . b . . . w . . . w . . .

MARY LAMB. The boys ought to write.

PATTY. John.

MARY LAMB. I set my brother's coach on fire. He died of fright. The horses dragged him through the town in the burning coach. It set light to the trees and houses. Over the bridge. I watched from my upstairs room. Sparks flying over the water. The coachman jumped. Coat on fire. Splash. Then out of the town. Horses rearing. Screaming. Through the lanes. Over the fields. Till it was all ashes. I said it was the lightning.

NAPOLEON. She tries to impress. Her brother died of drink years ago. I ruled Europe. The pope handed me the crown like a waiter and I put it on my head.

MILTON. Does Mr Clare still write?

MARY LAMB. He did at one time. Hundreds of ballads. Songs. I copied them into a book. His terrible hand! A scribble! No one paid me. You could send me some soap.

PATTY. Well you've got a lot of friends here John. Plenty t'talk about. Mind you share the apple jelly round. On't hog it. (*Slight pause.*) On't better stop. Tire you out. They'll be bringin' your teas round. On't git in people's road when they're workin'. If I can help it.

CLARE. L...l...

MARY LAMB. You look all right.

PATTY. Yes, well.

CLARE. G...g...

MARY LAMB. Grey hair.

PATTY. On't git younger. P'raps I'll see you again some time. Never know. Anyone told me last week I'd be here I'd a laughed. Sorry you on't had a proper life. Us hev t'make the most of what there is. On't us, boy? No use lettin' goo. (*Pats his arm.*) Learn some way t'stay on top. I'd be a fool t'cry now. 'Bye, 'bye.

> PATTY *goes through the open door in the windows.*

MILTON. Don't know why I said that about my son. Not true. Does his duty. Means very well. Scrupulous in fact. She's missed the cab.

> MILTON *hurries out through the open door in the window. Silence.* DOCTOR SKRIMSHIRE *runs in.*

DOCTOR. Is that Lord Milton going? How distressing. Clare have you made trouble?

> The DOCTOR *hurries out through the open door in the windows.*
> *He disappears. His voice is heard immediately.*
> (*Off, calling*). Lord Milton. The tea.

End

# CLARE POEMS

## CULTURE

All men must answer in their lives
Those questions whose answers are enormous
Because when one man decides how he lives
    He changes all men's lives

There are no small questions for small men
All men are Hamlet on an empty street
Or a windy quay
All men are Lear in the market
    When the tradesmen have gone

No man eats sleeps or loves for himself alone
Harvest and dreams and teaching the young
Don't take place in a small room
    But in the spaces of other men's lives

How we eat decides justice
Our homes measure the perversion of science
Our love controls the meaning of words
And art is whatever looks closely
    In the human face

If there were only irrational ways
To make the world rational
Art would still be reason
    And so our race not left to rot in the madhouse

Reason is the mark of kin
Poetry destroys illusions and doesn't create them
And hope is a passion that will not let men
    Rest in asylum's peace

# DARKIE AND THE MEN HANGED AT ELY

No work
Empty bellies
Wet houses
For charity the cold face of the fen

Duties: step out of the carriageway
Pray on sunday
Wait for a war to be paid to kill yourself

What happens?
Resist not evil?
Even the rat that eats a child's face?
We strike the rat away

For that they hang us
Like meat on a butcher's hook
While the judge chews his toothpick
His men harvest with a footpad's knife
For them reason is a sense of shame

When the untaught go quietly at the teacher's heels
To the grave
Love does not spring up in the rank shadow of the gallows
To cast out evil

Reason is armed when men cast out reason
For if driven from her home in the human face
She takes up refuge in the human fist

So say the five illiterates hanged at Ely

## ON ENTERING PARADISE

If tomorrow the gates of paradise flew open
When you touched them
It would still have cost much blood
    To open them

Look behind you down the long sluice
Of blood and debris of war past time
And remember this when a voice calls
    How shall we open the gates of paradise?

Blood of itself is not enough
Even in the veins to keep a man alive
And spilt it will not make history
    *That* is the work of reason

But whenever the tongue of reason is cut out
Then violence rises like a madwoman over her toys
Reason is not reborn from her own ashes
Prometheus has been saved a thousand times
    By the vulture that tears his liver

Remember this when you stand at the gates of paradise
And a voice calls from the sluice

## PATTY'S SPEECH

Small and bent lower
Round shoulders in black
Hands boney and clean
As poorman's knife and fork
Her face blank as a scraped plate
Helped by the neighbours since she is stricken
Sometimes she repays in jam
    From the fruit of the medlar tree

She goes to church to be counted
And never to the pub
And all her talk is cliches
A laugh to the carriage trade
A scandal to the schoolmaster
    Absurd in the theatre

Her words are worn steps outside
Stone offices
For her to be articulate would be
Impertinence to a master so skilled in mastery
He uses words to prove language has no meaning
    So the parson brays and the judge gnaws his lip

As she shuts the gates on the asylum
She doesn't speak of incarceration
Her thoughts are muffled by careful footsteps on the gravel
If asked she would say:
I make do with what I have and go without what I haven't
And no man can snap her

## MARY

A dark woman heavy as earth
Or light as shadows blown in wind

Who?

The woman you bought a ticket for on a bus
Or met once at the foot of a bridge
While the water made a hollow sound in its channel
Like a man under an operation

Not seen for twenty years
You are still taut from touching her

Who?

She is the woman you slept with last night
Who eats at your table
The mother in your house
Who welcomes guests at your door

But you and she are deformed
They tell you: this vacuum is cast for you
So fill it – as if the coffin were the human mould

No, all nature abhors what fills their spaces
The law that watches your bed
The butcher who waits at your table
The pedant waylaying your child at the school door

They took your wife
Now they will take your woman
You are a poet and should have known
You must imagine the real and not the illusion

She will age with your wife's silence
And your dreams bare in shrivelled wombs
The imbecile children who play in senile men

Your woman spent her life under your roof
You never met – not once
In the living room or kitchen
Clare, you created illusions
And they destroy poets

# AUTOBIOGRAPHY OF A DEAD MAN

Who am I?

I am the play of light
That looks in shadows
Some are as black as crime
In others I see
    The innocent in their cells

I am the comet
That runs over the night
As a madman
Having the shape of fire
    That breaks and creates

I am the light that goes
Through the machine
Till each steel face
And knot of iron
    Shines as the human face

I know Darkness
When black hands cup the flame
And the night wind howls
    To empty the world

I sat in the asylum chewing bread
I sang: The Sun is a Loaf
Outside it got greyer and people hungrier
If you are still alive and eat
    Remember

The starving decide the taste of your bread
Prisoners who is free
And the poor the nature of power

So I learned in my cell
And my dark friend in his
    That one day our bread might taste of reason

# WE COME TO THE RIVER

*We Come to the River* was first performed in English at the Royal Opera House Covent Garden on July 12, 1976, with the following cast:

GENERAL Norman Welsby
AIDE Paul Hudson
FIRST SOLDIER Francis Egerton
SECOND SOLDIER Gerald English
THIRD SOLDIER Alan Watt
FOURTH SOLDIER Malcolm King
FIFTH SOLDIER Alexander Oliver
SIXTH SOLDIER John Lanigan
SEVENTH SOLDIER Richard Angas
EIGHTH SOLDIER Dennis Wicks
MAY Elizabeth Bainbridge
NCO Bryan Drake
DESERTER Robert Tear
FIRST LADY Teresa Cahill
SECOND LADY Anne Pashley
THIRD LADY Joan Davies
FOURTH LADY Patricia Payne
FIRST GENTLEMAN Arthur Davies
SECOND GENTLEMAN John Barrow
THIRD GENTLEMAN Brian Donlan
RACHEL Deborah Cook
DOCTOR Michael Langdon
FIRST WHORE Jean Bailey
SECOND WHORE Elizabeth Shelley
THIRD WHORE Gillian Knight
WO John Winfield
FIRST WOUNDED Adrian de Peyer
SECOND WOUNDED David Lennox

THIRD WOUNDED Brian Kemp
FOURTH WOUNDED Eric Garrett
OLD WOMAN Anne Wilkens
YOUNG WOMAN
    Josephine Barstow
FIRST MADWOMAN Teresa Cahill
SECOND MADWOMAN Joan Davies
THIRD MADWOMAN Anne Pashley
FIRST MADMAN John Winfield
SECOND MADMAN
    Alexander Oliver
THIRD MADMAN John Lanigan
FIRST ATTENDANT Richard Angas
SECOND ATTENDANT
    Dennis Wicks
FIRST MINISTER Kenneth Bowen
SECOND MINISTER
    Tom McDonnell
THIRD MINISTER Michael Follis
SECOND SOLDIER'S WIFE
    Valerie Masterson
EMPEROR Josephine Veasey
GREY-HAIRED MINISTER
    George MacPherson
GIRL
FIRST ASSASSIN Adrian de Peyer
SECOND ASSASSIN David Lennox

---

SOLDIERS, NCOS, OFFICERS, OFFICIALS, LADIES, GENTLEMEN, WOUNDED, DEAD, GIRLS, MAD PEOPLE, TWO SENTRIES, CHILDREN

Paul Arden-Griffith, Ivor Bennon (accordionist), Antonia Butler, David Cusick, Raimund Herincx, Angela Hickey, Terry Jenkins, Yvonne Kenny, Gary Kettel (drummer), Julian Littman, Felicity Lott, Wyndham Parfitt, Susanna Ross, John Wakefield, Hilary Wilson (harpist), David Wilson-Johnson.

Music by Hans Werner Henze
Produced by Hans Werner Henze
Designed by Jürgen Henze
Conducted by David Atherton

## Europe: nineteenth century and later

The sections bracketed together should be played wholly or partly together.

# ONE

*HQ.*

GENERAL's *tent. Dark, quiet. Candles. An* OFFICER *sits at a desk ready to write. The* GENERAL *dictates. His words are split into groups so that the* OFFICER *can write them down.*

GENERAL. Sir I have to report victory. The – enemy are routed, all – survivors pursued and taken. The rebel army no longer exists. I – am sending the leaders to the capital –

> *Loud noises from the* SOLDIERS *in the canteen* (Section Two).

GENERAL (*calls*). Captain. (*Dictates.*) A first count puts –

> *The* AIDE *comes in.*

GENERAL. That noise?
AIDE. The men celebrating sir.
GENERAL. Stop them. Full alert will be maintained. Sentries will be posted. There are still groups of enemy survivors.
AIDE. Sir.

> *The* AIDE *goes.*

GENERAL. – puts our losses at twenty two thousand dead and wounded. No – rebel figures are to hand. Your – army behaved with valour. I – deem it necessary that your majesty appoints a – strong governor to this – province so that all further – opposition is immediately crushed.
I – am your majesty's obedient servant.


# TWO

*Canteen.* SOLDIERS *celebrating. Drink, smoke, movement.*

SOLDIERS. In the green green grass we lay
As on a lovers' bed
I'll love you Maggie May

While the grass is green I said
O Maggie you were sweet to me
But the grass is wither-ed
  O Maggie Maggie May
  They have taken you away
  For to stay on Van Dieman's cruel shore

FIRST SOLDIER. I put the bayonet through him. He bit on his fag and the wind kept it going. There he was sitting up dead with a fag burning.

SOLDIERS. Whose turn to order?

THIRD SOLDIER (*arguing with* FOURTH SOLDIER). He should have moved his troops left. We'd have been cut to pieces.

FOURTH SOLDIER. Bloody daft.

SOLDIERS. Beer.

*An* OLD WOMAN *called* MAY *comes in with a tray of beers.*

FOURTH SOLDIER. Where's your daughter May?

MAY. What's wrong with me?

*The* SOLDIERS *laugh.*

SECOND SOLDIER. Do this, do that, at the double. I'm sick of beer and blood.

FIRST SOLDIER. What will you do?

SECOND SOLDIER. Get out of the army. Marry and have children. I'll get up in the morning and there'll be no killing that day. I'll work hard. It'll be cold, it'll rain – but there'll be no killing. I'll be happy as long as no one tells me to kill and then bury what I've killed.

FIRST SOLDIER. You can't get out. You *will* work hard, it *will* be cold, it *will* rain. Your wife will always be tired. You'll have eight children and three will live. (*The* SOLDIERS *laugh quietly.*) And *they'll* be as thin as prisoners of war and walk like wounded soldiers.

MAY. Let him try.

THIRD SOLDIER (*still arguing*). They should have dug in by the river. Then they'd have stood between us and the hills.

FOURTH SOLDIER. Bloody daft.

THIRD SOLDIER. If he'd cut us off from the river –

FOURTH SOLDIER. Bloody daft.

> THIRD AND FOURTH SOLDIERS *fight. Others join in.* MAY
> *tries to stop them.*

MAY. Not on my premises. Out. Out.
SOLDIERS. Hit him. Kick him. Break his neck.
MAY. My glasses.

> *The* AIDE *and an* NCO *come into the canteen.*

AIDE. Out.
NCO. Out. Out.
MAY. Who's paying for my glasses?

> *The* SOLDIERS *hurry out.* NCO *stops the* FOUR SOLDIERS.

NCO. You – you – you – and you. I've got a job for you.

> *The* FOUR SOLDIERS *look at each other.*


# THREE

*Court martial.*
GENERAL'*s tent. Still night.* GENERAL, AIDE *and* OFFICERS. *The*
DESERTER *is marched in by the* NCO. *He is escorted by the* FOUR
SOLDIERS.

NCO. Escort and prisoner halt one two.
OFFICER. Name rank and number.
DESERTER. Dawson private 22743694.
AIDE. Prisoner deserted in the face of the enemy sir. He was
    found sitting by the roadside. When asked what he was doing
    he made no reply. Whereupon he was taken into custody sir.
OFFICER. Anything to say?
DESERTER. I – I – (*Stops.*)
GENERAL. Were you afraid? The guns, smoke, screaming horses,
    the big wounds? I understand, I've fought in the front.
DESERTER. I – I –
GENERAL. I was afraid too. You think I can let you go because

we've won. There *is* no victory – you only win time you need
to prepare for the next war. It will come, and the soldiers will
want to run away – they always will. I must make them stay.
You will be shot in the morning.

DESERTER. Sir – I –

NCO. Prisoner and escort right turn. Quick march one two.

NCO, DESERTER *and the* FOUR SOLDIERS *march out.*

## FOUR

*Assembly Rooms.*
*Local assembly rooms.* LADIES *and* GENTLEMEN *in formal dress.*
*The* LADIES *carry laurels. Polished table with glasses and wine.*
AIDE *and* OFFICERS *come in. The* GENERAL *arrives.*

FIRST GENTLEMAN. We are delegates of local society.

FIRST LADY. We honour your great victory.

SECOND LADY. And the victor.

RACHEL. We are patriotic daughters of the nation.

GENERAL. It is our privilege to serve his majesty.

*The* GENERAL *shakes hands with some of them.* RACHEL
*faints for a few seconds.*

FIRST LADY. My daughter Rachel, sir. She has composed verses
for the occasion.

RACHEL (*recovering*). They are entitled 'Hail Liberator'.

LADIES (*sing*).  Hail master of war
Hail bringer of peace

Clouds sweep over the battlefield
Over the sacrifice
It is an altar for the fatherland

God has granted the prayer
Uttered by the gun
He gives peace to the fatherland

Children will bless the warrior's old age
You have guarded their laughter
With the sword

Hail protector
Hail giver of freedom and laughter

GENERAL. I accept your tribute on behalf of my officers and men.

> GENTLEMEN *fill the glasses. They drink a toast.*

GENERAL. The emperor.
REST. His majesty.

> *As they sing the* DOCTOR *walks into the* GENERAL'*s tent (see Section Five). He is dressed in black. He sits and waits silently in the gloom.*

GENERAL. Ladies and gentlemen, excuse me. I must go back to my work.

> *The* GENERAL *goes alone.* CIVILIANS *and* OFFICERS *dance formally. The* CIVILIANS *leave when the dance finishes.*

LADIES AND GENTLEMEN. Goodnight. Our thanks. Goodnight.

> *The* OFFICERS *are left.*

CAPTAIN. I've ordered your whores, gentlemen.

> CAPTAIN *whistles.* THREE WHORES *come in.*

FIRST WHORE. Stinks of cow.
SECOND WHORE. Like a farmyard.
THIRD WHORE. Moo. (*They all laugh. Drunk and maudlin.*) Lieutenant Jones had his legs shot off.

> *The* OFFICERS *laugh.*

CAPTAIN. Major Hillcourt, comfort the lady.

> THIRD WHORE *lies on the table. She lifts up her skirts and the* MAJOR *gets on top of her. The other* OFFICERS *stand round in*

*a group and raise candelabras over their heads. It suggests romantic pictures of officers listening to girls playing the piano.*

THIRD WHORE. Both legs. Such a nice boy . . .
OFFICERS. When our schooldays are over
          We will meet
          And live the dreams
          We are dreaming now

          In the ocean
          Who hears the spring?
          In the deep
          Who hears the waterfall?

## FIVE

*Guard Room.*
*Small, bleak room.* DESERTER *and the* FOUR SOLDIERS *standing or sitting on the floor. One mattress.*

FIRST SOLDIER. Keep an eye on him. I'm going to kip.

    FIRST SOLDIER *lies on the mattress.*

THIRD SOLDIER. Cards.
DESERTER. No.
SECOND SOLDIER. Want the padre?
DESERTER. No.
FOURTH SOLDIER. No family?
DESERTER (*shrugs*). No.

    *Slight pause.* FOURTH SOLDIER *takes out a pack of cards.*

FOURTH SOLDIER (*to* DESERTER). Mind?
DESERTER (*shakes head*). No, go ahead.
FOURTH SOLDIER (*shuffles pack. Apologetically*). It's a long wait.

    FOURTH SOLDIER *deals.* SECOND, THIRD *and* FOURTH SOLDIERS *play.*

SECOND SOLDIER. What a hand! (*Sorts cards in disgust.*) Why did you run?

DESERTER. I don't know. They came out of the trenches and ran towards us firing with fixed bayonets. I ran. Then I found myself out on the road. I couldn't go back. Too late. So I sat down under a tree at the side of the road and waited.

FOURTH SOLDIER (*to* SECOND SOLDIER). Are you playing that card?

THIRD SOLDIER (*offers cigarettes to* DESERTER). Smoke?

> DESERTER *and* SECOND, THIRD *and* FOURTH SOLDIERS *take cigarettes and light them.*

SECOND SOLDIER. Your people dead?

DESERTER (*shrugs*). Don't know. I was brought up in a home.

FOURTH SOLDIER. Three of clubs.

DESERTER. A sort of barracks. Nine hundred children. Even the food smelt of children. We slept in a high room . . . If I hadn't sat under the tree and waited, if I'd run away! Are you a good shot?

SECOND SOLDIER. Yes.

DESERTER (*touches his forehead*). Shoot here.

FIRST SOLDIER (*angrily turning on the mattress*). This bed's got stones in it.

DESERTER. There were big windows high up in the walls. The children couldn't reach them – but we could always see the sky. When the sun shone you couldn't see the window frames. So bright! When there were storms the clouds went so fast – dark clouds, like bruises. They were so far away but they seemed to touch the house –

> FIRST SOLDIER *sits up furiously.*

FIRST SOLDIER. Wrap it you nut! By chriss I'll enjoy making a hole in you tomorrow.


# SIX

*Doctor.*
GENERAL's *tent. Still night. A few candles. The* GENERAL *comes in. The* DOCTOR *is waiting. He stands.*

GENERAL (*slightly puzzled*). Doctor?

DOCTOR. How is your head sir?

GENERAL. Fine.

DOCTOR. Any headache?

GENERAL (*dismissive*). It's nothing.

*The* GENERAL *sits. The* DOCTOR *sits after him.*

GENERAL. Urgent, doctor? Perhaps tomorrow . . .

DOCTOR. It's difficult. You once took a wound in the leg.

GENERAL. Back of the knee. No more than a boy in those days. Just entered the service of the emperor. Sometimes it's a bit stiff – a stick for a few days sees me through.

DOCTOR. It's difficult to explain. When you look at a battlefield you see things I can't. You send troops somewhere and the effect spreads – I can't see it but you can. Suddenly it affects another part of the field, far away, hours, days later. It decides victory and defeat.

GENERAL (*uncertain*). Go on.

DOCTOR. The wound behind your knee has worked in the same way. You are going blind.

*Pause.*

GENERAL. How soon?

DOCTOR. I don't know.

GENERAL. When?

DOCTOR. I can't say. Tomorrow, or it may be months.

GENERAL. Blind? Totally?

DOCTOR. Yes.

GENERAL (*trying to control himself*). What can you do? You must do something!

DOCTOR. There is nothing.

GENERAL. But surely –?

DOCTOR (*interrupting*). Nothing.

GENERAL. Nothing. (*Slight pause.*) Is it certain?

DOCTOR. Yes.

GENERAL (*angrily*). Nothing's certain. If it happens like – an

accident – surely something can stop it? Anything! Another
accident, a stroke of luck! Surely?

DOCTOR. When you look back you know the moment when a
battle was lost. It's like that. It was decided long ago. And now
the consequences have to be lived through. Shall I give you
something to make you sleep sir?

GENERAL (*coldly*). No, no. By no means.

DOCTOR. Shall I send for the padre, or your aide?

GENERAL. Goodnight.

*The* DOCTOR *goes. The* GENERAL *sits at his desk, hesitates
and then rings a bell. An* OFFICER *comes in.*

GENERAL. I shall finish my despatches to the emperor.


# SEVEN

*Execution.*

DESERTER *and the* FOUR SOLDIERS *standing in the guard room.*
NCO *enters.*

NCO. Sort yourselves out lads.

DESERTER. Where are we going?

THIRD SOLDIER. Behind the hut.

DESERTER. I thought they'd let me off!

SECOND SOLDIER. I'll cover your eyes. Best do it now, before
you go out. Lean on me. You'll be all right.

*SECOND SOLDIER covers the DESERTER's eyes and ties his
hands behind his back.*

NCO. Sharp lads.

DESERTER. Perhaps they'll change their minds. Let's hang on a
bit.

SECOND SOLDIER. No big parade this time. It won't take long.

NCO. Prisoner and escort quick march one two.

*They all go outside the hut. The SOLDIERS are not in step.
SECOND SOLDIER positions the DESERTER in the centre of
the empty space. No stake.*

SECOND SOLDIER. Stand there a moment.
DESERTER. Are we there?

> *The* SOLDIERS *are moving quietly away from the* DESERTER.
> *They unsling their rifles.*

SECOND SOLDIER. No. We've got to hang on here a bit.
DESERTER. Yes, yes – let's hang on. Give them a chance to
change their minds.

> *The* SOLDIERS *start to aim, carefully and quietly. At the same
> time the* AIDE *and other* OFFICERS *come in.*

SECOND SOLDIER (*reassuringly to* DESERTER). That's right, hang
on.
AIDE (*shouts to* NCO *and points to* SECOND SOLDIER). Tell that
man to be quiet.
DESERTER (*spinning round to face the* AIDE). Who's there?
AIDE (*to* NCO). You're in charge here. The punishment will be
carried out in the proper soldier-like manner.
NCO (*to the* DESERTER *as he staggers away*). Attention.
AIDE. Still!
SECOND SOLDIER. Shoot!

> *Immediately the* FOUR SOLDIERS *shoot raggedly, and* FIRST,
> THIRD *and* FOURTH SOLDIERS *shout 'Shoot!' once as they
> shoot. The* DESERTER *falls dead. The* NCO *marches to the
> body, stops, looks down, turns to the* AIDE *and salutes.*

NCO. Punishment correctly carried out sir.
AIDE (*salutes*). Thank you sergeant.
> (*Points to* SECOND SOLDIER.) Charge him.

> AIDE *and* OFFICERS *go out.*

NCO (*to* SECOND SOLDIER). You're on a charge lad: talking on
parade.

> *The* NCO *and the* SOLDIERS *go out with the body.*

## EIGHT

*Fatigue.*

WO *stands on one side of the parade ground. Smartly dressed, carries a swagger stick.* FOUR SOLDIERS *sweep the parade ground. They wear fatigue dress. They move in line. The four brooms are exactly alike: long white handles and heavy heads with coarse, long bristles.*

WO. Move as one man. I like to see men smart when they sweep. (*Goes to a* SOLDIER *and stops him.*) Look how you hold your tool lad! Get a proper grip. Right arm bent smartly at the elbow attaching itself firmly to the handle in an area approximating to your right breast with the left arm extending down the length of the handle and the left hand firmly attached to a level approximating halfway down your left thigh and with both thumbs extending along the length of the handle and not curled round it like a pig's tail so as to direct the broom-head over the area desirous of being a-swept with the maximum cleansing effect whereby you swing the right elbow up and pull the left hand smartly in towards your body in one good soldier-like action.

> *The other* SOLDIERS *have stopped to watch. He turns to them.*

Is this our meditating hour? Have we joined the happy band of the little yellow Buddha?

FIFTH SOLDIER. No sir.

> *The* WO *goes to a part of the parade ground that has been swept. More* SOLDIERS *come on and erect a saluting stand (see Section Ten).*

WO (*pointing to the ground*). D'you call that swept lad?

EIGHTH SOLDIER. It's cleaner than it was sir.

WO. Get off! Get off my parade ground with your dirty boots!

> *The* SOLDIERS *start to hurry off. The* WO *calls after them.*

Scrub the handles before you hand the brooms into stores. Use soap and water! I like my brooms to have a good clean soldier-like handle on them.

*The* SOLDIERS *hurry out. The* WO *flicks at dust on the parade ground with a white handkerchief.*

Swept?

*The* WO *goes out.*

## NINE

*Battlefield.*
WOUNDED *and* DEAD. *A few cry. The* GENERAL *comes in immediately. He walks over the battlefield and then stands very still. He doesn't look round.*

FIRST WOUNDED. I'm lying on my leg. I can smell it . . .
SECOND WOUNDED (*delirious*). Look at the birds. Why are they so still?
THIRD WOUNDED. Who's there? Are they taking us away?
FOURTH WOUNDED. Who won? . . . Who won? . . . Who won?

*The* GENERAL *shuts his eyes and listens. Two* WOMEN *come in, one old and one young. The* YOUNG WOMAN *brings a heap of rags. She points at the* GENERAL.

YOUNG WOMAN. Is that him?
OLD WOMAN. No, no. Too old.

*The* OLD WOMAN *goes to* FIRST WOUNDED.

FIRST WOUNDED. Help me. I can smell my leg. It's rotting.
YOUNG WOMAN (*looking at* FIRST WOUNDED). Is that him?
OLD WOMAN. No. (*Searches through* FIRST WOUNDED's *pockets.*) Empty! Someone's been here before us.
THIRD WOUNDED. Help. Help.
YOUNG WOMAN. Take his boots.
OLD WOMAN. They've gone. Help me get his jacket.
SECOND WOUNDED. The birds. Still.
FIRST WOUNDED. Be careful. My leg. It's rotting.
OLD WOMAN (*taking the jacket*). This jacket's full of blood, that's

why they left it – but they cut the buttons off. (*She tries to lead the* YOUNG WOMAN *away*.) Quickly, it's dangerous here.

YOUNG WOMAN (*looking back at* FIRST WOUNDED). I thought I recognized his voice . . .

FIRST WOUNDED. My leg.

*The* YOUNG WOMAN *suddenly stops and points at the ground.*

YOUNG WOMAN. Look, an arm in the ground. Buried soldiers.

OLD WOMAN. We must dig them up. There might be something left on them.

*The two* WOMEN *start to scrabble out the buried soldiers.*

GENERAL. Blind. Blind. Blind. I shut my eyes and hear things moving round me. Is it the wind? (*He opens his eyes.*) Blindness has been creeping through me for years like a spy.

FIRST WOUNDED. I can't feel my legs. What's happening?

SECOND WOUNDED. The birds. Waiting. Still.

FOURTH WOUNDED. Who won? . . . Who won? . . . Who won?

*The* YOUNG WOMAN *suddenly crouches over a half dug out soldier.*

YOUNG WOMAN. It's him!

OLD WOMAN. No, no.

YOUNG WOMAN (*scrabbling to get the body out*). It's him!

OLD WOMAN. Don't!

YOUNG WOMAN. My darling! Look how they've broken your face!

OLD WOMAN (*running to the* GENERAL). Help me. My daughter.

*The* GENERAL *goes to the* YOUNG WOMAN *and tries to pull her away.*

GENERAL. Don't! These bodies are full of disease.

YOUNG WOMAN. This is my husband!

GENERAL. Absurd! How can you tell? Look, there's no face. He could be anyone. His clothes are anyone's – a uniform.

YOUNG WOMAN. I know his hair.

GENERAL (*pulling her away*). Then you know him! (*He suddenly becomes icily cold. He lets her go.*) So you know he's dead, you know he's buried. So what can you do? Nothing. There are thousands of dead men here.

YOUNG WOMAN (*stands still and stares at the* GENERAL). What did he say? . . . (*She looks at the body.*) He was my husband. (*Looks at the* GENERAL *again.*) I can't understand him . . . No, *you* can't understand *me*! Have you killed so many men, seen so many bodies? You don't know what you look at any more! (*She goes to the heap of rags and picks out a baby.*) Our child. Look, asleep. (*Showing the baby to the* GENERAL.) A different thing: sleep, not death. (*Gently.*) Sleep. Sleep.

GENERAL. Take her home. She is mad. (*Turns angrily to the* YOUNG WOMAN.) I killed no one. They are war dead. They gave their lives.

YOUNG WOMAN (*looking down at the child*). Let me show you to your father.

GENERAL. That's not his father!

YOUNG WOMAN. No, perhaps not. But he could be. His father looks like that now. (*She sits by the dead body, nurses the child and holds the dead soldier's hand.*) I shall sit here and hold his hand. When it turns to bone I will cover it with my own hand.

*The* AIDE, OFFICERS, NCOS *and* SOLDIERS ONE *to* SIX *come in.*

AIDE. Sir the new governor has arrived.

GENERAL (*to* YOUNG WOMAN). You will make the child ill.

OLD WOMAN (*crying*). Let me take him away.

AIDE. Sir the governor.

GENERAL. The governor? I must go back. It is discourteous . . . (*His voice trails off as he stares at the* WOMEN *and the* CHILD.)

AIDE (*to* SOLDIERS). Get rid of these looters.

GENERAL. No! Leave them . . . The governor, it is discourteous . . . (*He turns away from the* WOMEN *and the* CHILD.) . . . to make him wait.

*They all go except the* WOMEN, CHILD *and* WOUNDED. *The* WOUNDED *call. The* OLD WOMAN *cries.*

## TEN

*Governor.*
*The* GOVERNOR *stands in front of the saluting stand. He is dressed*
*formally but he mixes informally with the* LADIES *and* GENTLEMEN
*who have come to meet him and he shakes some of them by the hand.*
*At the same time* SOLDIERS *are being paraded with regimental*
*colours and a military band.*

GOVERNOR. The emperor is deeply moved by the role of the
civilian community in this struggle.

FIRST GENTLEMAN. We did our duty.

SECOND LADY. No more.

FIRST LADY. It is for us to set the example to the army.

THIRD LADY. All my daughters have studied nursing.

RACHEL. If they'd attacked our towns we would have fought
them on the streets.

GOVERNOR. I shall personally inform the emperor of your
sentiments.

FIRST LADY. Only our duty.

SECOND LADY. No more.

SECOND GENTLEMAN. The emperor's proclamation against the
rebels inspired us.

THIRD LADY. A torch.

THIRD GENTLEMAN. We shall defend our homes and families.

RACHEL. If they'd attacked our houses we would have fought
them over the rooftops.

*During this the* WO *parades the colour party of six* SOLDIERS.

WO. Colour escort number.

SOLDIERS. One. Two. Three. Four. Five. Six.

WO. Even numbers one pace to the rear, odd numbers one pace
to the front move. Colour escort left turn. (*To* OFFICER).
Colour escort paraded sir.

*The* OFFICER *marches to join the colour escort. The*
GOVERNOR *goes onto the saluting stand.*

OFFICER. Parade present arms.

> *The colour salute is played. Spectators stand to attention. The* GOVERNOR *salutes. The* SOLDIERS *present arms. The colours are dipped. During this the* GENERAL *and the* AIDE *hurry on. When the salute ends the* GOVERNOR *turns to the* GENERAL.

LADIES. Hail. Hail.

GOVERNOR. General the emperor sends you his grateful thanks. The whole nation is indebted to you.

FIRST LADY. He is numbered among the nation's heroes.

SECOND LADY. The glorious pages of our history.

GOVERNOR. When the military situation permits you will be summoned to receive thanks directly from his majesty's hands.

LADIES. Hail. Hail.

GENERAL. She said I've seen so many bodies I don't know what I look at any more.

GOVERNOR. The emperor has entrusted this province to my care.

FIRST LADY. We shall rest safely in his hands.

FIRST GENTLEMAN. You shall command our loyal duty.

SECOND LADY. Our uttermost respect.

FOURTH LADY. He shall lead us through the dangers.

RACHEL. Hail protector
          Hail giver of freedom and laughter

GENERAL. And then she said sleep, not death. (*Gently.*) Sleep. Sleep.

AIDE (*to* GENERAL). Sir, the governor . . .

GENERAL (*looks round*). What are these people doing? There are wounded men dying in the fields. (*He turns away from them again.*) Sleep, not death?

AIDE (*touching the* GENERAL's *arm*). Sir what is the matter?

GOVERNOR. What is wrong?

FOURTH LADY. He says wounded men are dying.

FIRST GENTLEMAN. The wounded are being attended to.

SECOND GENTLEMAN. Rescue parties are at their side.

THIRD LADY. My daughters trained in nursing.

SECOND LADY. I gave linen.

FIRST LADY. He said sleep, sleep.

RACHEL. God has answered the prayer
          Uttered by the gun
GENERAL. You see, I was not prepared: the old woman cried.
I've seen the strong cry, but not the weak. Why wasn't I
prepared to see how the weak cry?

*The* GENERAL *goes out.*

GOVERNOR. Ladies and gentlemen this assembly is ended.
Go home. An announcement will be made. Do not spread
alarm.

*The* LADIES *and* GENTLEMEN *start to go.*

LADIES AND GENTLEMEN. What did he say? The weak cry?
He looked so foolish, like a servant who's dropped a plate.
There will be an announcement. Go quietly home. No alarm.

*The* LADIES *and* GENTLEMEN *go out.*

DOCTOR (*to* GOVERNOR). Sir the general is going blind.
REST (*shocked and quiet*). Blind.

*Everyone goes.*


# ELEVEN

*Battlefield.*
*The* YOUNG WOMAN *sits with the* CHILD *at her breast. She holds
the* SOLDIER's *hand in one hand. The* OLD WOMAN *sits a little
away and watches her. The* YOUNG WOMAN *sings to the child.*

YOUNG WOMAN. Five sticks and an apple
          One head, two arms, two legs
          Stick them in: a man
          Throw him, catch him, play
          When you're hungry: eat him

*The* GENERAL *comes in.*

GENERAL. The soldiers will follow me. I'll try to save you but perhaps they won't obey me now. Let her take the child away . . . The father's seen it . . .

YOUNG WOMAN (*hands* CHILD *to* OLD WOMAN). Bring him back when he's hungry – or if he cries.

*The* OLD WOMAN *goes out with the* CHILD.

GENERAL. Why did you come here?

YOUNG WOMAN. To loot. This is the only way we can live. Everything we had is gone.

GENERAL. But why are you sitting with . . . a dead stranger?

YOUNG WOMAN. My husband worked hard but there wasn't much to eat. Sometimes he drank and then he got angry. It didn't matter. We were happy. He'd never lay away from me in bed, he always turned to me . . . (*She holds the* GENERAL.) Then they cut his hair and put him in a uniform. He looked so strange when he came to say goodbye. He stood in the door-way and tried to smile. But he looked so awkward. I cried.

AIDE, NCO *and* SOLDIERS *come in.*

YOUNG WOMAN. He put his rifle on his back but it fell off when he kissed me.

AIDE. Sir the soldiers are asking questions. This is bad for morale.

*The* GOVERNOR *and* DOCTOR *come in.*

GENERAL. Go away. I'm not a soldier now. I've left the emperor's service.

DOCTOR. Symptoms of shock.

GOVERNOR. Who is this woman?

AIDE. Prostitute sir.

GOVERNOR. And a looter? Have her shot.

GENERAL. She's under my protection. I order you to –

GOVERNOR (*interrupting*). You cannot give orders. You said it yourself: you have left the emperor's service. Shoot her.

AIDE (*to* SOLDIERS. *Points upstage*). Over there.

SOLDIERS *go to the* YOUNG WOMAN.

GENERAL. No!

GOVERNOR. It was your order, issued before the fighting! Looters, spies, deserters – all to be shot.

AIDE (*to* SOLDIERS). Quickly.

GENERAL. I beg you. I served the emperor all my life. I gave him my eyes. I ask for so little now.

GOVERNOR. Every civilian witness of this sordid affair must be removed.

*The* SOLDIERS *take the* YOUNG WOMAN *upstage.*

YOUNG WOMAN. Where is my husband? Are you taking me to him?

FIRST SOLDIER. Come here.

THIRD SOLDIER. Over there.

YOUNG WOMAN (*struggling*). I saw him then! Where is he? Is it you? Or you? Is he hiding? Hold me!

*They shoot her twice in the head with a pistol. She falls dead.* FIRST, SECOND, THIRD, FOURTH *and* SIXTH SOLDIERS *go out.*

GENERAL (*remotely*). Two shots. Two sounds fly over the trees and a heap of rags falls to the ground. Her blood runs over the stones and the law is stronger by one more death, the armed men are stronger by the strength of one woman who was too mad to know who they were . . .

GOVERNOR. Tie him and take him back to camp.

*They tie the* GENERAL*'s hands behind his back.*

He must be sent to a house for the insane. It must be made clear that these are the acts of a madman and do not reflect on the emperor.

*They all go except an* NCO *and* FIFTH *and* SEVENTH SOLDIERS. *They put the body of the* YOUNG WOMAN *in the grave with the dead soldier and kick dirt over them. They go out.*

## TWELVE

*River.*
*River with a line of stepping stones between two banks. The* OLD
WOMAN *sits on one bank and nurses the* CHILD *in her lap.*

OLD WOMAN. Nibble my finger. Go on, you won't get much out
  of it. It's a dry old stick. We'll find a spring in the rocks somewhere. Perhaps there's a goat hiding up there with her kid.
  She'll give you milk. A clever goat that hasn't been shot . . .

> FIRST, SECOND, THIRD, FOURTH *and* SIXTH SOLDIERS
> *come onto the bank behind her and sit down quietly. The* OLD
> WOMAN *stands with the* CHILD.

FIRST SOLDIER. Toss a coin?
THIRD SOLDIER (*shakes his head*). No – we're all in this one.
OLD WOMAN. You're young enough to be my grandsons. Let us
  go. No one knows you've found us.
FOURTH SOLDIER. They make you do things no one should even
  have to dream of and cheer you when you've done it.
THIRD SOLDIER. They'll moan and complain.
SIXTH SOLDIER. Keep on at us.
SECOND SOLDIER. There's no way out once the order's given.
OLD WOMAN. I've held the child so quietly he doesn't know
  you're here. He doesn't even know you're fighting.

> *The* OLD WOMAN *has begun to cross the stepping stones. On
> the second stone she turns and looks at the* SOLDIERS. *They
> sit motionless on the bank with their rifles cradled in their laps.*

OLD WOMAN. They'll think we're dead. I won't let you down –
  no one will find us.

> *The* OLD WOMAN *crosses over more stones. The* SOLDIERS
> *don't move. She stops and looks at them.*

OLD WOMAN. It was wrong of me to let you catch us. That
  makes it so difficult for you. (*She bows to the* SOLDIERS.) We
  apologize to the soldiers. (*She looks at the* CHILD.) You're old
  enough to be his father. Look, he's still smiling.

AIDE, GOVERNOR, DOCTOR, GENERAL, NCOS *and*
SOLDIERS, *including* FIFTH *and* SEVENTH, *appear on the
far side of the river. The* GENERAL's *hands are tied behind
his back. The first group of* SOLDIERS *spring to their feet.
The* OLD WOMAN *retreats back to the middle stepping stone.*

AIDE. What are you men doing?

FIRST SOLDIER. Winded sir.

THIRD SOLDIER. Had to chase her sir. Getting our breath
back.

AIDE. Fools! (*To* OLD WOMAN.) Give me the child.

OLD WOMAN. No.

AIDE. There's no point in having it killed. I'll have it cared for.

OLD WOMAN. Cared for? (*Violently.*) The men who killed my
daughter, burned my house, made me hungry and cold and
filled me with despair and hate – *they* were in your care, and
what have you done to them?

SOLDIERS *begin to step along the stones towards her. They
come from both sides.*

OLD WOMAN. Go back.

FIRST SOLDIER. Careful.

THIRD SOLDIER. Wildcat.

FIFTH SOLDIER. Bitch.

OLD WOMAN. Go back.

FOURTH SOLDIER. Cow.

FIRST SOLDIER. Pig.

OLD WOMAN. Go back.

FIFTH SOLDIER. Sow.

*A* SOLDIER *reaches out for the* CHILD. *The* OLD WOMAN
*holds it above her head.*

OLD WOMAN. This child has no voice. I curse you with his
voice. With the curse of children. With the pain of children.
You should father no children. They will be born old and
white and dead.

GENERAL. I curse you with the voice of children. With the
death of children. You should father no children. They will

be born old and white and dead. With hands red from your crimes. With eyes dazed from your violence. With fingers writhing like strangler's rope. Their breath will stink of your victim's graves.

GOVERNOR. Let him rave. The more who hear him now the better.

DOCTOR. Symptoms of madness. Anxiety. Depression.

OLD WOMAN. They will be born without hope. Their voices will be your victim's cries.

*The* OLD WOMAN *jumps into the river with the* CHILD. SOLDIERS *run up and down the stepping stones and the river banks trying to see her in the river. They point and give staccato shouts.*

THIRD SOLDIER. There she is.

FOURTH SOLDIER. That's the child.

FIFTH SOLDIER. A bundle.

FOURTH SOLDIER. It's moving fast.

SECOND SOLDIER. Round and round.

AIDE. Shoot them.

FOURTH SOLDIER. A bundle of rags.

FIRST SOLDIER. She's pulling it under.

THIRD SOLDIER. That's the current.

SECOND SOLDIER. She's holding onto something.

FIFTH SOLDIER. On the bottom.

FOURTH SOLDIER. Trying to drown.

AIDE. Shoot them.

*The* SOLDIERS *move and shout as before. They start to take pot shots at the water with their rifles.*

SIXTH SOLDIER. That's them.

FIRST SOLDIER. Got her.

THIRD SOLDIER. Weeds in the water.

SIXTH SOLDIER. She's coming up.

FIFTH SOLDIER. Spinning round.

THIRD SOLDIER. It's broken up.

FIRST SOLDIER. Things in the water.

FOURTH SOLDIER. That's the kid.

SIXTH SOLDIER. Upside down.

FIRST SOLDIER. There's its feet.

FOURTH SOLDIER. A piece of wood.

SECOND SOLDIER. A white sheet in the water.

AIDE. Shoot them. Rake the water.

*A* SOLDIER *stands on each of the stepping stones. They fire several volleys straight down into the water. The water hisses and splashes.* SOLDIERS *stand on the banks and watch. The* GOVERNOR, DOCTOR, GENERAL *and* OFFICERS *go out.*

AIDE. Enough. Conserve your ammunition. It has to be paid for.

*The* SOLDIERS *move off the stones. They stand in a loose untidy group on the bank and watch the* AIDE *looking down into the water. He sees them.*

AIDE (*to* NCO). Sort them out.

NCO *gestures in annoyance to the men. They form into a ragged order and trot out with the* NCO. *The* AIDE *takes a last look at the water and then follows them out. The sound of the current and frightened water birds.*

## *Part Two*

### THIRTEEN

*Garden.*
*Madhouse garden. The* MAD PEOPLE *are quiet, slow and withdrawn. They move like clouds on the tops of mountains. Many of them sit in isolation and sing monologues. (These are given in an appendix.) During this other* MAD PEOPLE *start to build an invisible boat.*

GENERAL. Voices! Voices!

FIRST MADWOMAN. My eyes are blinded by the light on the water.

SECOND MADWOMAN. Let's go to the island. Get in!

MAD PEOPLE *start to get into the boat.*

FIRST MADMAN. Get in. Get in.
GENERAL. Day and night! Voices!
THIRD MADMAN (*to* GENERAL). Come to the island.
GENERAL (*not moving*). Voices!
THIRD MADMAN (*angrily to the* GENERAL). Come to the island!
Come to the island!

*The* MAD PEOPLE *raise invisible sails and the boat moves off.*

MAD PEOPLE. The boat goes over the water
Birds fly from the broken sea
The iron chain drops to the deep
Like a silent killer

Here in the light tears dry on my face
I feel the wind in my mouth
My child's hands are small
I cannot turn keys or lift burdens
But I must pull the heavy oars
So that the boat goes fast through the water

SECOND SOLDIER *enters. He wears shabby civilian clothes.*

FIRST ATTENDANT (*looking up from his book*). Yes?
SECOND SOLDIER. I am visiting my father. (*Shows document.*)
My pass. (*Points.*) Is that the general?
FIRST ATTENDANT. What if it is?
SOLDIER. I was in his headquarters. Can I speak to him?
FIRST ATTENDANT (*looks at the* SOLDIER *for a moment, then answers*). You won't get anything out of him. (*Laughs and goes back to his book.*)

SECOND SOLDIER *goes to the* GENERAL.

SECOND SOLDIER. General. Do you know what is happening outside?
GENERAL (*softly*). More voices.
SECOND SOLDIER. There is no work and we are hungry.

GENERAL. How long have I been here?

SECOND SOLDIER. There are riots in the streets. The soldiers take men to the barracks and torture them. They will not let us pass their buildings because we hear the cries.

GENERAL. They say there is an island in a river.

SECOND SOLDIER. How can the prisoners stop the torturers? They are not torturing to get information or the truth. There's nothing you can tell them that will stop them. They torture because they have been ordered to: that is all. And the torturers are too afraid to ask why.

GENERAL. The river has dried up. I sit on the empty river bed in the hot sun. A lizard lies and pants in my shadow. When I move it drops into the dark crack in the earth.

SECOND SOLDIER. No one talks in the streets now. Friends smile quickly and pass by. No one helps their neighbour. What if their neighbour is arrested next week? Then they will be arrested for helping the enemy.

GENERAL. They say they will sail away, the cool wind will fill their sails and take them to their island. No! – the sun is god's torture in the sky.

SECOND SOLDIER. They break musicians' hands and runners' legs. Fathers go to work and vanish. Mothers go to shop and they are never seen again. They say there are too many people anyway. They send you an official document and a little box of ashes.

GENERAL. When you are mad the sun stops at mid-day.

SECOND SOLDIER. The people write your name on the walls. You are their hero: you attacked the emperor. None of the leaders had spoken against him before! Help us now. Tell us what we shall do.

GENERAL. The sun is hurting my eyes. They have locked me in this house where the sun always shines. My eyes are burning! My head is on fire! These voices are like flies! Tell them there is no river! No island! The river is dead!

*The* MAD PEOPLE *murmur angrily.*

MAD PEOPLE. He says there is no island. He says there is no river. He's destroying our island. We must have our island.

We are happy there. Peaceful and free. (*They come towards the* GENERAL *and threaten him.*) He destroys our island! You take the river away! Kick him! Hit him! Throw him in the river!

FIRST ATTENDANT (*running over. To* SECOND SOLDIER). Get out! You're making trouble!

SECOND SOLDIER *goes.* FIRST ATTENDANT *pushes the* MAD PEOPLE *away.*

FIRST ATTENDANT. Get back to your river. Go and play in your boat. It's a beautiful boat! Be quiet or you'll be locked in your rooms.

*The* MAD PEOPLE *go back to the river murmuring.*

MAD PEOPLE. He's destroying our island. He's taking our river away. Warn him. Warn him. Warn him.

*The* MAD PEOPLE *get into their boat.*

FIRST MADMAN. Not one cloud.
MAD PEOPLE. Grass grows on the river bank
           Rain pours over the white roots
           Into the water

FIRST MADMAN *jumps out of the boat.* THIRD MADMAN *throws him an invisible rope.* FIRST MADMAN *catches it and ties it to a tree.*

GENERAL. Voices saying nothing!
MAD PEOPLE. Watch the river wander
           Over fields
           Hiding under bridges

*The* DOCTOR *comes in with the* GOVERNOR.

DOCTOR. How are your eyes sir?
GENERAL. I can see.
DOCTOR. Strange. Symptoms develop slowly in you. But you will go blind.
SECOND MADMAN. How beautiful by the river.
THIRD MADMAN. The river holds its finger against drowned
    's mouths. It is a noose to strangle the general.

GOVERNOR. General, the emperor sends his greetings. He has excused your past conduct. You were under stress. Now there is more fighting in the provinces. Civil war. The emperor orders you to return to the head of his army. Not to take decisions – I can tell you that privately. We need your moral, symbolic support. This is a time for national unity. You will take salutes, read speeches and present medals. Use the last of your sight to serve your emperor!

GENERAL. Feel the lines on my face. Am I so old?

DOCTOR. You see, his condition is worse.

GOVERNOR. You have been shut up so long. When you leave here you will get better. We are not asking much in return for your freedom.

GENERAL. Freedom! I'm not so blind I can't see why you're here! I'm not so mad I can't understand why they sent you! You are so desperate that you've come to me! Have *all* the people turned against him at last! Tell the emperor you can do nothing to save him! Nothing! What does he want us to do? Shed more blood? No! If he sheds any more his own soldiers will drown in it!

DOCTOR (*to* GOVERNOR). I warned you, sir.

GOVERNOR *and* DOCTOR *go out.*

GENERAL (*to himself. Afraid*). Dangerous, dangerous – to say those things to them. Like reasoning with a madman. Every night I dream. There is nothing to see – only the darkness of sleep. But I am dreaming. I stand still and very quiet. I hear things moving in the darkness, groping, calling my name. And in my dream I am watching myself when I am awake. (*Calls to the* ATTENDANT.) The doctor. Fetch the doctor.

FIRST ATTENDANT (*not looking up from his book*). We're not your servants now.

MAD PEOPLE. See the trees stretch over the river
　　　　　No hand comes from the water
　　　　　To put fruit on their branches.

FIRST ATTENDANT (*looking up at the* MAD PEOPLE). Don't get excited.

# FOURTEEN

*Assassination.*
*This section is in three parts which overlap.*
*A) Government room. The* GOVERNOR *sits at a table with the*
AIDE *and* THREE MINISTERS. *Lamps. Dark outside.*

GOVERNOR. My mission to the general failed. His mind has
gone. He can't help us. There is worse news from the mountains. Our army is trapped between precipices, rivers and
passes. Staff officers out-manoeuvred by peasants!

AIDE. The general staff is not to be insulted!

GOVERNOR. Crack regiments rubbed out by schoolboys!

AIDE. The emperor's soldiers fought like heroes!

GOVERNOR. They fought each other like rats – to run away over
the bridges and scuttle down passes. Whole armies vanished
into the hills.

AIDE. They had nothing to fight with! They were let down by
the people at home. How can we fight without weapons and
ammunition?

FIRST MINISTER. Industry is reluctant to invest. The war has
lasted too long. No decisive victories – and no decisive defeats –
creates a lack of confidence.

AIDE. You sent loyal men to be slaughtered!

SECOND MINISTER. The situation at home has deteriorated.
Violence on the streets. Crime. It's not safe to go out.

THIRD MINISTER. Food prices up and up. If we're not defeated
at the front we'll be defeated at home. Some of the people
are so obstinate they'll starve before they spend their
savings!

MINISTERS. Casualties mount and profits rise
  → But the best of all possible worlds has a flaw
  Dead soldiers cannot use guns
  What are we to do? Careful!
  God grant us perfection
  Give us the lion's hunger and the patience of the
    spider

A national day of prayer!
Stop shouting – my head aches!
The will to win!
Cowardice! Betrayal!
Hear hear!
Time is running out!
O god where have we gone wrong?

SECOND SOLDIER *comes to the gateway outside the meeting room. He wears his uniform and carries a rifle. He stands to attention like a sentry.*

GOVERNOR. The emperor demands stronger measures. If we don't act we'll all be kicked out. A permanent pool of hostages will be maintained and a suitable number shot in response to the slightest provocation or outrage.

AIDE and MINISTERS. Yes.

SECOND MINISTER. And we mustn't quarrel among ourselves.

THIRD MINISTER. No, there's too much at stake.

AIDE and MINISTERS. Yes.

*B) Gateway outside the meeting room.* SECOND SOLDIER *stands at attention in the dark.*

SECOND SOLDIER. I stand here like a sentry. Lights on in their room. It looks empty. No one comes to the window. They're sitting round the table murdering my children under the electric light. What do children ask? Mother where do the birds fly? Father why is the grass green? Why does the sea play all day? Why are the mountains so far? No, our children ask: Father why are we cold? Mother why are we hungry? Father why are the streets so quiet except when the bands march by? Father why are the houses so grey except when they hang them with flags? Father what are you afraid of? Father why do they pile bombs on the corner of the street? Father why are the soldiers wiping their knives again? Father why do people sit in squares in the park all day, why have they brought those bundles? Father why do you get up in the night and stare out of the window at the empty street? Father answer! . . . He will come down soon.

*C) Slum room.* SECOND SOLDIER'*s* WIFE *stands alone. The three* CHILDREN *sleep on a low bed.*

SECOND SOLDIER'S WIFE. He watches the children play and talks to them like a kind stranger. I woke up in the night and he was lying so still in the dark with his eyes open. I asked him why couldn't he sleep but he didn't answer. He got out of bed and stared through the window at the empty street. Since they took him away he has been silent. How can I help him? He sees me crying and nods and touches me. But he can't speak. Now he's gone to find work – but why did he wear his uniform? The children ask so many questions. They give him no peace. I try to answer for him – but what can I tell them? – the world is as big as the giant in their fairy book, but it's too weak to feed little children? They are young, but the world is an old, old witch who gives birth to throw children to the prince's hunting dogs?

*B) Gateway outside the meeting room. The* GOVERNOR *finishes signing papers. He leaves the meeting and hurries out into the dark. He salutes* SECOND SOLDIER *as he passes.* SECOND SOLDIER *shoots him. The* GOVERNOR *falls.* SECOND SOLDIER *looks at him and runs out. A moment's silence. Voices are heard off.*

MEN'S VOICES (*off*). Who fired? A shot!

    OFFICERS *run in.*

FIRST OFFICER. O god, the governor.
SECOND OFFICER. Dead?
THIRD OFFICER. Alert the barracks.
OFFICERS. He's hit! The heart! His head! Guards. Stop him bleeding! Help! A doctor! Where's the sentry!

    MINISTERS *hurry from the meeting room.*

FIRST OFFICER. O god his excellency the governor is dead.

    *The* MINISTERS *stoop over the body.*

FIRST MINISTER. Take hostages. The governor signed the order before he died. His last human act. He fights our enemies beyond the grave.

SECOND MINISTER (*to* THIRD MINISTER). We must clear out. It's all finished here.

THIRD MINISTER (*to* SECOND MINISTER). It will all collapse. We'll go abroad.

OFFICERS *carry the body out.*

*C*) *Slum room.*

SECOND SOLDIER'S WIFE. So late. So late.

SECOND SOLDIER *comes in.*

SECOND SOLDIER'S WIFE. Where have you been?

SECOND SOLDIER. Are the children asleep?

WIFE (*angrily*). Where? Where? Where? Why did you take your uniform?

SECOND SOLDIER. The children. Don't wake them.

WIFE. Please don't go back to the army. Please don't leave us.

SECOND SOLDIER (*quietly*). Quiet. The children.


# FIFTEEN

*Court.*
*Riverside picnic. White sheets, glasses, silver, porcelain, bottles, food. The* EMPEROR *is young, handsome, healthy and vaguely exotic – like an Indian prince educated at Oxford. He wears a black jacket and pale trousers.* TWO SENTRIES *in court uniform. A* GREY-HAIRED MINISTER. GIRLS *in white, blue and green dresses.*

EMPEROR (*relaxed*). One of my provincial governors has been shot. The killer had paid a visit to my mad general.

GREY-HAIRED MINISTER. People write your mad general's name on your palace walls.

GIRL. Will you have him tried?

EMPEROR. Can I try a mad man?

GREY-HAIRED MINISTER. You must do something. The people call him their hero. Some of them would like to put him in your place.

EMPEROR. Yes. I must do something. I'm too old to be afraid of anything but my own death.

GIRL. Old? Death?

EMPEROR. Why doesn't he go blind? They promised me he would. That would be the best solution. Even my enemies wouldn't follow a blind leader . . . The obstinate old fool.

*The* GIRLS *wander away. They are anxious.*

GIRLS.   The beautiful little white clouds
        Are baskets of silver fish
        The bright sun
        Has an iron hook in its mouth

        Every night the pale moon rises
        A ghost
        Weeping and wandering over the polar snow
        Hiding from the sun

EMPEROR. Everyone must solve one thousand problems in his life. Then he dies. One thousand, for the cook and the emperor. An old emperor solved nine hundred and ninety-nine problems. Then he went to hide in the mountains. Many years passed. Buddha heard of this holy man and went to see him. The hermit's door was locked. Buddha banged on it and the hermit covered his head with a shawl. He banged again. The hermit crept under his blanket. Then Buddha beat on the door with his holy stick very hard and the stick broke. Buddha wept. The hermit heard the god weeping. (*The* GREY-HAIRED MINISTER *pours champagne.*) He ran to the door and knelt reverently before the god. Buddha said 'What shall I do? I must walk round the earth to comfort the hungry and afflicted. It's a long way and I shan't get far without my stick. Help me. I am a god and so I cannot work.' Sadly the hermit picked up the pieces of the Buddha stick and bound them together and on that day he died.

GIRL (*laughing awkwardly*). Why do you say you are old?

EMPEROR. I have solved nine hundred and ninety-nine problems. Now I shall blind the general and send him a white stick to show my innocence.

## SIXTEEN

*Madhouse.*

*Two blocks too heavy to be moved by the* MAD PEOPLE. FIRST ATTENDANT *sits on the smaller block and reads his book. The larger block is empty. The* DOCTOR *comes in.*

DOCTOR. The governor has been shot.

GENERAL. When? Who shot him? Is there a new governor?

DOCTOR. So many questions.

GENERAL. Is there a new governor?

DOCTOR. No. Martial law.

GENERAL. And reprisals?

DOCTOR. I don't ask questions. I choose to live in seclusion with my patients. They have the man who shot him. Can you guess who it was?

GENERAL. No.

DOCTOR. I think you can. The soldier who came here. He said he was visiting his father. That was a lie. He'd forged a pass. He came to see you.

GENERAL. Where is he now?

DOCTOR. He was in a room with his wife and children.

GENERAL. Yes?

DOCTOR. The soldiers sealed it off.

GENERAL. Go on.

DOCTOR. He shot himself. And his wife and children. They were dead when the soldiers broke in.

GENERAL. How many children?

DOCTOR. More questions?

GENERAL (*grabs the* DOCTOR. FIRST ATTENDANT *moves forward*). How many children were shot?

DOCTOR. Three. I think.

GENERAL. I was promised blindness and madness and death! Let me put out my eyes!

*He tries to destroy his eyes with his hands. The* DOCTOR *and* FIRST ATTENDANT *struggle with him.*

DOCTOR. Jacket. Jacket.
GENERAL. O god let me go mad!

SECOND ATTENDANT *runs in with a strait-jacket.*

FIRST ATTENDANT. Get his legs.
DOCTOR. Jacket. Jacket.
GENERAL (*struggling and shouting as they put him into the strait-jacket*). I see things that should make me blind! I live in a cage – that should make me mad! I've lived long enough to earn death! Young men die. Mothers die. Children die. Why must I live on and on?
FIRST ATTENDANT. Straps.
SECOND ATTENDANT. The bastard kicks.
GENERAL (*becoming calmer*). I will sit, I will sit.

*The* GENERAL *sits on the large block. The* ATTENDANTS *fasten him to it with a short chain at the back of the strait-jacket.*

DOCTOR. Breathe. These disturbances soon pass. Breathe.
GENERAL. When will I go mad or die? You promised me long ago I would go blind. How much more must I see? I wait and do nothing – but I still destroy. The soldier came to me and I sent him away. Now he is dead. All my life I have increased the number of dead. Even at the end. Is it so difficult to vanish off the face of the earth? I am like an evil ghost that upsets the hands of the clocks other men live by.

TWO ASSASSINS *come in.*

FIRST ASSASSIN. Where is the general?
DOCTOR. Who are you?
SECOND ASSASSIN (*pointing to* GENERAL). That him?
DOCTOR. Who are you?
FIRST ASSASSIN. Leave us alone with him.

DOCTOR. No. He's my patient. I can't leave him in this condition.

FIRST ASSASSIN (*hands letter to the* DOCTOR). Read your instructions. It refers to 'all possible assistance'.

DOCTOR *reads the letter.*

SECOND ATTENDANT (*whispering*). What do they want?

FIRST ATTENDANT (*whispering*). Listen.

*The* DOCTOR *nods to the* TWO ATTENDANTS *and goes out with them. The* ATTENDANTS *glance back as they go.*

FIRST ASSASSIN. Shut all your doors please.

SECOND ASSASSIN *goes upstage to make sure the doors are shut.*

GENERAL. I sit here like an ox tied to the slaughter-house door. If there was still a sky I would lift my head and roar at it. (*Laughs.*) O Maggie May! Sergeant Major, why are the men singing?

SECOND ASSASSIN (*coming back*). All shut.

FIRST ASSASSIN (*admiringly*). Like his suit.

SECOND ASSASSIN. Natty.

FIRST ASSASSIN. Convenient.

SECOND ASSASSIN. A joke really.

FIRST ASSASSIN. Can't shake his hand before he goes.

SECOND ASSASSIN. Smile so he has something pretty to remember.

FIRST ASSASSIN *takes out a knife.*

SECOND ASSASSIN. My turn, I think.

SECOND ASSASSIN *takes the knife from* FIRST ASSASSIN. FIRST ASSASSIN *holds the* GENERAL'*s head.* SECOND ASSASSIN *draws the knife neatly across the* GENERAL'*s eyes. The* GENERAL *struggles.*

Still. Hold him.

GENERAL. Ah!

*The* TWO ASSASSINS *step back.*

FIRST ASSASSIN. Did it work?

SECOND ASSASSIN. Don't like it. Should have used a gun on him.

GENERAL. Ah! If there was still a sky I would lift my face to it! O Maggie Maggie May!

> FIRST ASSASSIN *moves his hand in front of the* GENERAL'S *eyes.*

SECOND ASSASSIN. Blind.

> *The* ASSASSINS *go. As the blindfold is put on the* YOUNG WOMAN *appears in the distance. She carries the* CHILD. *The* GENERAL *doesn't see her at first. She comes nearer.*

GENERAL (*groans*). Ah! Sergeant Major tell the men to bring me the sky.

YOUNG WOMAN (*she uncovers the* CHILD *and looks at it*). Smile. Father's working. He will soon be home. Along the path, through the trees, by the gate, and up to the door.

GENERAL. My eyes! What has happened to my eyes? I see such beautiful things.

YOUNG WOMAN (*to* CHILD). Father has planted trees for you. He will show you how to climb them.

GENERAL. I killed you. I signed the paper.

> *The* DESERTER *comes in.*

DESERTER. I'm late. I was tired and I sat down by the road to rest. How is the child? (*The* DESERTER *takes the* CHILD.)

YOUNG WOMAN. He's smiling now.

GENERAL. The deserter. I shot you too. Look, there's blood on your head. Answer my questions. Tell me! Will the world go mad? Will a terrible sun burn it till it is a desert littered with dead? Answer me! Let me be sane before I die. I wanted to be buried in a huge square under a stone man on a stone horse. Now I would like to lie under trees by running water where there is still a sky.

> *The* OLD WOMAN *comes in.*

GENERAL. The old woman. They shot you in the water. Your wounds were washed as they were made. Answer my question.

*The* OLD WOMAN *takes the* CHILD *from the* DESERTER.

DESERTER. Gentle.

*The* OLD WOMAN *sings to the* CHILD.

OLD WOMAN.
Shall I tell you who is weak?
The weak buy men for riches
And sell them for famine
They paint flowers on the
    desert and call it a garden
They smile like the torturer
    and bow like the judge
They lead armies to hell so
    that they shall have a
    kingdom to rule in

Shall I tell you who is
    strong?
Child, you are strong
You have nothing and your
    hands are small
But the world spins like clay
    on a potter's wheel
And you will shape it with
    your hands

*The* YOUNG WOMAN *takes the* CHILD *from the* OLD WOMAN *and lays it on the ground. She arranges its wrappings so that it is comfortable.*

*Other victims come slowly on stage.* SECOND

*The* DOCTOR *comes back with the* TWO ASSASSINS.

FIRST ASSASSIN. Doesn't look good to me.
SECOND ASSASSIN. Blind.
DOCTOR (*to* GENERAL). I'll give you something for the pain.
SECOND ASSASSIN. He's all cracked up.
DOCTOR (*threateningly*). I shall report this to the emperor.
FIRST ASSASSIN. The medical certificate will do.

*The* DOCTOR *and* ASSASSINS *go out.*

GENERAL.
The world spins like clay
    on a potter's wheel
And he will shape it with
    his hands

SOLDIER, *his* WIFE *and* THREE CHILDREN, SOLDIERS *and* PRISONERS. *They are all wounded, with blood-stained bandages or wounds. As they come on they join in singing to the* CHILD. *The song lasts till the end of the opera. It accompanies the incidents around the* GENERAL.

### Song of the Victims

Child from the river
The water has rocked you
The reeds kept the wind
    from your head
The wind has sung to you

Child you have slept so still
    by the river
The earth was a pillow
    under your head
The reeds have kept the cold
    winds from you
And man stood watch over
    your bed

Child do not whimper in
    your sleep
The dark ice melts in the sun
The rain runs into the river
Spring has begun

*The* MAD PEOPLE *start to drift on. The* GENERAL *looks towards the* CHILD.

FIRST MADMAN. Rain runs over the white roots.
FIRST MADWOMAN (*looking at the* GENERAL). Why are you staring?
THIRD MADMAN. The boat! The island!
SECOND MADWOMAN. Let's sail to our island!
FIRST MADWOMAN. What's happened to his eyes?
SECOND MADMAN. He's staring at us.
SECOND MADWOMAN. Stop it! Stop it!
THIRD MADMAN. He's a spy!
SECOND MADMAN. I'm afraid!
MAD PEOPLE. A spy. A spy.
FIRST MADWOMAN. I'm frightened of him!
THIRD MADMAN. He'll take our island away! He wants to destroy our river. Spy. Spy. Spy.
THIRD MADWOMAN. Drown him!
MAD PEOPLE. The water! The river! Drown him!

MAD PEOPLE *run to get white sheets and white blankets to use as water.*

*They attack the* GENERAL.
*They push him over and*
*smother him with the*
*sheets and blankets. The*
GENERAL *struggles as if*
*he was fighting waves.*

## Song of Three Dead Children

The soldiers shot us
Bang bang you're dead
Why does the wind still
    whistle
In the holes in our head?

*The* THREE DEAD
CHILDREN *look at the*
MAD PEOPLE.

FIRST DEAD CHILD. Look at
the funny people.
SECOND DEAD CHILD. Let's
go and play with them.
THIRD DEAD CHILD. No, we
must teach our new brother
how to sing.
ALL THREE.
    Ah. Oh. Listen to our voices
    How bright they are. How
    clear!

MAD PEOPLE. Drown him.
Throw him in the water.
Push him in the river.
Hold him under. He's
climbing out. Jump on his
hands. Hit him. Push him
back. Down. Under. Under.
I can't get at him. Drown
him. Hold him under the
water. Kill him. Head
down. It's in his mouth.
Stuff his mouth. Bubbles.
Drown his head. Drown
his arms. Drown his feet.
Drown his bones. Drown
his heart. Drown him.
Drown him. Drown him.
Drown. Drown. Let the
tide carry him out. Wash
him away. Hide him under
the river. Tie a stone on
his feet. Let him vanish
under the water. Hide him
quickly. Wash him away.

## Song of the Victims
*(continued)*

A white horse is nibbling
    the wet grass!
See the silk cradle on its
    back!
It waits by the path

*The* MAD PEOPLE *try to*
*cover the dead* GENERAL
*with the sheets and blankets.*

The soldiers marched by
in the night
Pink flesh in the steel shell
They are lying on the shore
The last order faded away
far out on the sea
Only the birds flying to land
heard it

The echo of guns dies on
the hills
Tatters of uniforms tumble
away in the wind
The chains of prisoners are
turned into chains for
anchors
Clowns dance where men
stood like sticks
Where the earth was trod
to dry circles they heap
flowers

We stand by the river
If there is a bridge we will
walk over
If there is no bridge we
will wade
If the water is deep we will
swim
If it is too fast we will
build boats
We will stand on the other
side
We have learned to march
so well that we cannot
drown

*The* DOCTOR *and the* TWO
ATTENDANTS *rush in.*

DOCTOR. Lock them up.
FIRST ATTENDANT. Cells.
Cells.
SECOND ATTENDANT. Out.
Out. Out.

*The* DOCTOR *and the*
ATTENDANTS *chase the*
MAD PEOPLE *away. A*
*small* MADMAN *and*
THIRD MADWOMAN *stay*
*by the dead* GENERAL.

SMALL MADMAN (*playing with*
*the sheets*). Whee! Woosh!
Splash! Splash!
THIRD MADWOMAN (*washing*
*her hands in the sheets.*
*Rubbing the sheets against her*
*cheeks*). O the water is clean
and cold and pure! How
beautiful I am! Beautiful!
Beautiful! Beautiful!
SMALL MADMAN. Whee!
Woosh! Splash!

SECOND ATTENDANT
*comes back and chases the*
SMALL MADMAN *and*
THIRD MADWOMAN
*out.*

*The* SINGERS *wander away. The dead* GENERAL *under the*
*sheets and the* CHILD *lying in its wrappings are left on stage.*

# APPENDIX

Monologues for Section Thirteen.

## ONE

The king had Raud brought to him. He offered him baptism and said 'I won't take your property, I'll give you my friendship – if you earn it.' Raud said he would never be a christian and he laughed at God. The king was angry. He said Raud should have the worst death. The king tied him to a horizontal beam with his face upwards. Then he forced his mouth open with a wooden wedge and stuck an adder in it. The adder shrank back when Raud breathed hard against it. So the king stuck a hollow branch of angelica root in Raud's mouth. But others say the king put the snake into his horn, put the horn in Raud's mouth, and forced the adder to go down with a red hot iron. Anyway the adder crept into Raud's mouth and down his throat and gnawed its way free out of Raud's side. So Raud died. The king took a lot of property – money, weapons, and other valuables. He baptized some of Raud's men and killed and tortured those who wouldn't be baptized.

## TWO

I and the children got a job helping with the harvest. For this we earned a quart of grain. Each meal was a handful of grain cooked up with some weeds. The children's bellies were swollen. and you could see their bones sticking through the skin. After a while the little boy couldn't get up anymore. He just lay on the k'ang. He had dysentery. Then the worms began to crawl out of his behind. A lot came out, one after the other. They were very thin and fell on the k'ang and wriggled. We collected them and got enough to fill a basin. Even after he died the worms kept wriggling out. The little girl couldn't get any milk from my breast because I had nothing to eat myself. She died too. Our neighbour worked in the fields with her children. A wolf came and they were too afraid to move. It took a big piece from the girl's leg. The boy cried. 'Look how big the wolf's mouth is. What a terrible red tongue.' Some men chased the wolf away but the girl died.


## THREE

A crowd of ten thousand went to Paras, Texas, in special trains to watch the execution of a mentally-retarded black man. He'd killed a little girl. They stuck red hot irons into his body, his eyes were burned out, hot pokers were pushed down his throat. After nearly an hour of this they set him on fire. Thousands came by excursion trains to Palmetto, Georgia, on a Sunday afternoon to see a black man burned alive. They cut off his ears, toes and fingers and passed them to the crowd while he was alive. Later they sold pieces of his heart as souvenirs. A black man charged with murder was tied to a stake on stage at the opera house in Livermore, Kentucky. Tickets for the performance entitled the buyer to help to kill him. People in the best seats were entitled to empty their revolvers in him, but people in the gallery were allowed only one shot. In Georgia a pregnant black woman was slowly roasted alive. Her baby was cut out and kicked around.


## FOUR

I then walked round the mound and found myself in front of a large grave. People were closely wedged together and lying on top of each other. Only their heads were visible. Nearly all had blood running from their heads over their shoulders. Some still moved. Some lifted their arms and moved their heads to show that they were alive. The pit was already two-thirds full. I estimated that it held a thousand people. I looked for the man who did the shooting. He was an SS man who sat at the edge of the narrow end of the pit, his feet dangling into it. He had a tommy gun on his knees and was smoking a cigarette. The naked people went down some steps cut into the clay wall of the pit and clambered over the heads of those lying there to the place pointed out to them by the SS man. They lay down in front of the dead and wounded. Some embraced the living and talked to them in a low voice. Then I heard a series of shots. I looked into the pit and saw that the bodies still twitched, or the heads lay motionless on top of the other bodies. Blood ran from their necks.

## FIVE

They saw a blinding white flash in the sky, felt a rush of air and heard a loud rumble of noise, followed by the sound of rending and falling buildings. All also spoke of the settling darkness as they found themselves enveloped by a universal cloud of dust. Innumerable fires burned unchecked for days. The city gave the impression of having sunk, in an instant and without struggle, to the most primitive existence. People directly under the explosion had their exposed skin burnt so severely that it was immediately charred dark brown or black: they died within minutes or at most hours. The symptoms suffered by others included nausea, vomiting, fever, bloody diarrhoea, general malaise and progressive anaemia. This last caused the thin blood to seep in small and large haemorrhages into the skin and the retina and sometimes into the intestines and kidneys. In severe cases the patient became infected. This usually spread from the mouth and was accompanied by gangrene of the lips, tongue and sometimes the throat. These deaths came from anaemia, internal bleeding and infection. Only about one-third of pregnant women gave birth to what appeared to be normal children.

## SIX

Arrived Matadi 13th June 1890. Feel considerable doubt about the future. Gosse gone with a large load of ivory down to Boma. Monday 30th. To Congo da Lemba after passing black rocks. Camp bed. Water far. 2nd July. District of Lunkungu. Great market at 9.30. Crossed low range of hills and broad valley. Met officer of State inspecting. Few minutes after saw dead body of Backongo. Shot? Horrid smell. NW.-SE. by low pass. Landscape gray-yellowish. Left camp 6 am. Dead body lying by path in attitude of meditative repose. Fell into muddy puddle – beastly! Fault of man that carried me. At night when moon rose heard shouts and drumming. July 7th. Lukunga Government station.

No water. Mr Davis returning from preaching trip. 29th. Wooded ravines. On road passed skeleton tied to post. Also white man's grave. Cold mists. 1st August. Mfumu Mbe. Government shanty. Row between carriers and man. About a mat. Blows, sticks. Stopped it. Youth with gun wound. Bullet entered inch above right eyebrow, came out a little inside roots of hair. Gave him a little glycerine to put on wound. Mosquitoes. Frogs. Very hot. Wind south.